This book belongs to

....

Bible
Stories

Retold by Vic Parker

Miles
Kelly

First published in 2017 by Miles Kelly Publishing Ltd
Harding's Barn, Bardfield End Green, Thaxted, Essex, CM6 3PX, UK

Copyright © Miles Kelly Publishing Ltd 2017

2 4 6 8 10 9 7 5 3 1

Publishing Director Belinda Gallagher
Creative Director Jo Cowan
Editors Carly Blake, Becky Miles
Designers Jo Cowan, Michelle Cannatella, Rob Hale
Consultant Janet Dyson
Production Elizabeth Collins, Caroline Kelly
Reprographics Stephan Davis, Jennifer Cozens
Assets Lorraine King

ISBN 978-1-78617-298-3

Printed in China

British Library Cataloguing-in-Publication Data
A catalogue record for this book is available from the British Library

ACKNOWLEDGEMENTS
Cover artwork: Aurélie Blanz

All other artwork is from the Miles Kelly Artwork Bank

Made with paper from a sustainable forest

www.mileskelly.net

The Bible is often described as the world's best-selling book, however it is more like an entire library. It is made up of sixty-six individual books, and split into two sections known as the Old Testament and the New Testament. The Bible is believed by countless readers all over the world to be the Word of God. It was written by many people over more than one thousand years, from about 1450 BC. Originally written in Hebrew, Aramaic and Greek, the Bible has been translated into many different languages.

CONTENTS

The Old Testament.............6-147
The New Testament........ 148-320

THE OLD TESTAMENT

The Old Testament is the name for the first section of the Bible, made up of thirty-nine books written over two thousand years ago. They were compiled by Jewish people who lived in the Middle East (where parts of Israel, Palestine, Lebanon, Syria, Jordan and Egypt are today). The books describe the Jews' special relationship with God over hundreds of years, beginning with the creation of the world. The Jews made many careful copies of the original ancient manuscripts, so the writings of the Old Testament were never lost. They contain family trees, religious laws, poetry, hymns and stories that narrate the events of hundreds of characters.

The Creation of the World 8

Adam and Eve in the Garden of Eden 15

Noah and the Ark 21

The Great Flood 25

Abram's Journey 30

God's Promise Comes True 38

A Terrible Test for Abraham 42

A Tale of Twin Brothers 48

Joseph the Dreamer 56

A Slave in Egypt 63

The Ruler of Egypt 69

The Silver Cup 73

The Baby in the Basket 82

The Burning Bush 88

The Nine Plagues of Egypt 94

The First Passover 102

Escape Across the Red Sea 105

The Ten Commandments .110

Joshua and the Battle of Jericho 118

Ruth the Loyal 124

David and the Giant 128

Solomon the Wise 134

Jonah and the Giant Fish 139

Daniel in the Lions' Den .145

The Creation of the World

In the beginning, God lived in darkness. There was nothing else except for a vast ocean that rushed and raged over a mass of land that lay beneath. Then God said, "Let there be light!" And there was. God liked the brightness. He enjoyed it for a while and then called the darkness back for another turn. That was the very first day and night.

When God lit up the second day, He began His next work. "I want a roof to arch over everything, way up high!" He said, and all at once there was one. Then He parted the ocean, scooped up half of the water and poured it out onto the roof. The swirling patterns that formed above were beautiful. God gave the roof a special name – sky.

God looked down at the remaining water boiling and bubbling below. "Move aside so the land can show through!" He ordered, and it did. The land rose up and the water swirled around it. God was very pleased and decided to call them earth and sea. God made this world even more beautiful with grass and flowers and bushes and trees. Before the third day ended, they were growing all over the earth.

On day number four, God decorated the sky. In it He hung a blazing, hot light called the sun, a pale, cold light called the moon and millions of burning, twinkling stars. Then He set them all moving around each other in a way that would mark out the passing of the days, nights, seasons and years.

On day five, God looked over His creation and began to fill it with creatures to enjoy His world. He spent the fifth day imagining all sorts of creatures that floated, swam and dived in the water, and that soared, hovered and buzzed in the air, and

it was so. The sea was filled with fish and sea creatures and the air was busy with birds and insects.

On the sixth day, God imagined creatures that galloped, hopped and slithered. Creatures with fur, scales and shells, and with claws, hooves and horns. Creatures that barked, hissed, howled and grunted. All at once, the earth was alive with all kinds of animals.

Last of all, God took a handful of earth and modelled it into a figure that looked just like Him. He bent down and breathed into the figure's nostrils. It shivered, blinked and came alive, and looked at Him. It was the first man, Adam. God saw that the man would be lonely all on his own, so He sent him into a deep sleep while He made him a companion. God gently took out one of the man's ribs and healed up the wound. Then He shaped the rib into another, similar figure – the first woman, Eve. Finally, God brought Eve to life, then woke up Adam and introduced them to each other. God watched His two humans with delight as they spoke and got to know each other. God was so thrilled with them that He put them in charge of all the other living things He had made. He even planted a beautiful garden especially for Adam and Eve to live in, in a place called Eden.

At last, God sat back and looked at the world He had created. He had used every colour, shape and texture, and every size,

sound and scent that He could think of.
God was very pleased with everything, and
He spent the seventh day resting after all
His creations. God blessed the seventh day
as a special day of rest in memory of when
He had completed His wonderful work.

And that is how the world was made.

Genesis chapters 1, 2

Adam and Eve in the Garden of Eden

God made sure that the Garden of Eden had everything that Adam and Eve needed to be happy. The sun kept them warm, so they didn't need clothes – they weren't embarrassed about being naked anyway. A gushing stream gave them water. All sorts of flowers, plants and trees grew

there, fragrant and shady, and
bearing tasty fruits, nuts and seeds.
In the middle of the garden grew
the two most beautiful trees of all – the
Tree of Life and the Tree of Knowledge.

"Take care of my marvellous garden,"
God told Adam and Eve. "Enjoy eating
anything you like, except for the fruits of
the Tree of Knowledge. Please do not eat
those. If you do, you will die."

Adam and Eve did as they were told and
their life in the garden was wonderful, until
one day Eve met a snake. The snake was by
far the most cunning of all the creatures
God had made. Very slyly, it asked Eve,
"Did God really tell you not to eat from
one of the trees?"

"Yes, that one," replied Eve, pointing to the Tree of Knowledge. "He said that if we do, we'll die. I don't think we're even allowed to touch it."

"Nonsense," hissed the snake. "You won't die! God doesn't want you to eat that fruit because if you do, you'll become like Him. You'll know the difference between good and bad, just as He does."

Eve gazed nervously at the Tree of Knowledge. How beautiful it was! Its leaves whispered mysteriously in the breeze and its branches stretched towards her. Its fruits hung down, ripe and ready to drop into her hand. "How wonderful it would be to become wise!" Eve murmured. Overcome with longing, she reached out, picked the nearest fruit and took a big, juicy bite. It was so delicious! Surely something that tasted so good could not be wrong. Eve hurried to share the fruit with Adam and he couldn't resist trying it either.

Suddenly, Adam and Eve realized that they did indeed know the difference between good and bad – and what they had done was very wrong. The couple felt dreadfully ashamed and were embarrassed about being naked too. They tried to sew leaves together to cover themselves. Then, in horror, they heard God coming. Quickly, they hid, but God knew.

"Adam," God called, "why are you and Eve hiding from me?"

The red-faced couple crept out, hanging their heads.

"We were frightened when we heard You, and also we weren't dressed," Adam mumbled.

"What has made you want clothes? And why are you afraid of me?" God demanded. "You haven't eaten the fruit I asked you not to eat, have you?"

Adam owned up, but he blamed it all on Eve, who in turn blamed the snake. God listened as they squirmed and squabbled. Then with huge disappointment He said, "I have no choice but to punish you all."

He sent the snake crawling away in the dust, the enemy of humans forever. After making animal-skin clothes for Adam and Eve, He turned them out of their beautiful garden home. "From now on, you will have to fend for yourselves and struggle to grow food," God told them. "And one day, you will go back to being the earth from which I made you – you will one day die." He set angels with fiery swords to guard the Tree of Life, so that Adam and Eve could not eat its fruit to save themselves from eventually dying. God watched in great sadness as the shamed couple walked out into the world.

Genesis chapters 2, 3

Noah and
the Ark

As the years went by, Adam and Eve's many great-great-grandchildren had many great-great-grandchildren of their own. People spread all over the world. They quite forgot that they were part of one big family. They also forgot about God and began behaving badly in all sorts of ways.

God looked down from Heaven and became more and more sad and angry. Eventually, people became so selfish and cruel that God was sorry He had ever created the human race. He decided the best thing was to remove everybody and start all over again.

Well, not quite everybody. There was just one person in the world who tried to live a good, honest, hard-working life – a farmer called Noah. God decided to save Noah, his wife and three sons, Shem, Ham and Japheth, and their wives.

God spoke to Noah and told him about His terrible decision. "Look around you, Noah. Everyone in the world is evil, and I have had enough. I am going to wash

everybody off the face of the earth, but I
promise, you and your family will be safe.
Here's what you have to do. I want you to
build a huge, covered boat – an ark. Use
the best wood you can find and build it
133 metres long, 22 metres wide and
13 metres high, with a roof of reeds. Coat
the whole thing with tar, inside and out, so
that it is watertight. Give it a door and
windows and build three decks divided into
compartments. When I tell you, load up the
ark with one pair of every living creature –
a male and a female. Take seven pairs of
animals you can eat because you'll need
enough food to feed you all. I am going to
send forty days and forty nights of rain to
flood the whole world."

Noah told his family and they hurried to begin the enormous task. Their neighbours thought they were mad as they began building the huge ship. How people laughed! But Noah and his family trusted God and kept working, and after many months the ark was finished. The day came when God warned Noah to begin loading the animals into the ark and settling his family onboard. A week later, thunder clouds blackened the skies, blotting out the sun, and it began to rain.

Genesis chapters 6, 7

The Great Flood

The rain that God sent to flood the world was like nothing anyone had seen before or could have imagined. It was as if the sky had shattered and through the cracks plunged mighty waterfalls. As the rain poured down, rivers burst their banks, lakes flooded their valleys, oceans swelled and overflowed and the ark floated off on the rising waters. Towering tidal waves rushed over the land, drowning everything in their path and still the rain continued. The ark was lashed and battered, and hurled this way and that by the currents.

The rain fell for forty days and nights just as God had said. Then as quickly as it had started, it stopped. When Noah dared to peep out, he could see nothing but water in all directions.

Over the quiet, empty days that followed, the sun began to dry up the water and the flood gradually started to sink. God sent a great wind to speed things along. Eventually, the ark groaned and shuddered as it scraped along the ground and came to a halt on top of Mount Ararat in Turkey.

Noah didn't dare leave the ark yet. He waited a few days for the waters to sink further, then sent a raven into the sky. The raven soared back and forth and all it could see was water. Noah waited a week, then sent out a dove. It flew back the same day and Noah knew that there was not enough land showing yet. He waited another week, then sent the dove out again. That evening it returned, carrying an olive leaf. The waters were low enough to show land where trees grew! Noah waited one week more and again sent out the dove. This time it did not return. Nervously, Noah opened the door and the ark was surrounded by dry land!

Then God called, "Noah, it's time for you and your family to go out into the world with the creatures and begin again." And that's what they did. God was pleased and blessed Noah and his family. He vowed that He would never again send a flood to destroy the living things He had created. God set a rainbow in the sky as a sign to always remind everyone of His promise.

Genesis chapters 7 to 9

Abram's Journey

One of the descendants of Noah's son Shem was a man called Abram. He grew up in a city called Ur, near the Persian Gulf. After Abram married he took his wife, Sarai, his father, Terah, and his orphaned nephew, Lot (whom he had brought up as his own son) to live in a northern city called

Haran. Both Ur and Haran were bustling places full of wealthy people just like Abram, who was a successful businessman. But one day, out of the blue, Abram heard God calling him.

"Abram, I want you to leave and go to the country that I will show you. I am going to make you the father of a great race of people."

It must have taken a lot of faith to do as God asked. Abram sold most of his possessions, packed up the rest and set off with his wife on a long journey without really knowing where he was going. Abram did it without questioning and talked Lot into coming too. He bought flocks of sheep, goats and cattle for himself and his nephew.

He hired shepherds too, and bought camels and mules to carry tents, belongings, food and water. After weeks of preparation, Abram led his family and hired helpers away from everything they knew, moving in a huge train south.

God led Abram down into the land of Canaan, which is now called Israel. When Abram reached

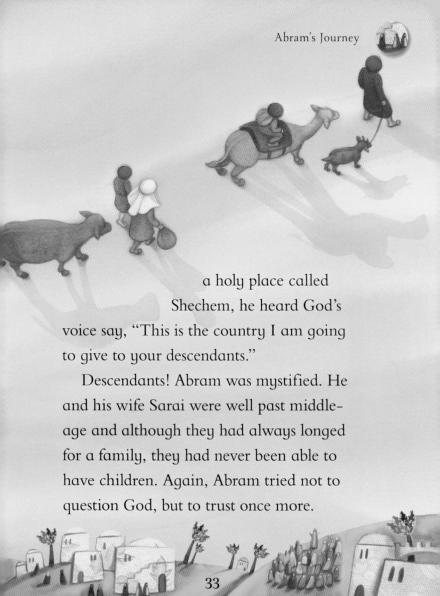

a holy place called
Shechem, he heard God's
voice say, "This is the country I am going
to give to your descendants."

Descendants! Abram was mystified. He
and his wife Sarai were well past middle-
age and although they had always longed
for a family, they had never been able to
have children. Again, Abram tried not to
question God, but to trust once more.

They could not stay in Canaan as there was a terrible famine, so God guided the family through the desert to the lush land of Egypt. Here, food and water were plentiful but Abram found himself in quite another kind of trouble. Pharaoh, the king of Egypt, ordered that Sarai had to become one of his wives. So God sent a terrible disease to strike Pharaoh and his advisors until he changed his mind, and he soon let Sarai go.

After that, Abram left Egypt behind and headed north into Canaan again to a place called Bethel. There wasn't enough grassland for all the animals to graze on, and Abram's and Lot's shepherds began quarrelling and fighting over it. There was only one thing for it – the two men split up.

Lot went east into Jordan where he settled at a city called Sodom, while his uncle unpacked his tents and stayed in the countryside of Canaan. After Lot had left, God spoke to Abram again and repeated his vow. "Look around you," He said. "All this land as far as the eye can see will belong to you and your family forever."

And so Abram waited... and waited... Seasons came and went, but there was still no sign that he and Sarai would ever have children.

Over the years, God spoke to him several times, repeating his promise. It was always when Abram least expected it. One night, Abram was sitting outside his tent as usual when he heard God say, "Look up. You will have as many descendants as there are stars in the sky." Another time, after Abram had made an offering to God, he had a terrifyingly real dream. In it God walked right next to him, vowing again that he would have a vast, wealthy family and that all the land from the River Nile to the River Euphrates would be theirs.

As time went on, Sarai grew concerned that she would never be able to give Abram a child so she encouraged her eighty-six-year-old husband to have a baby with her maid Hagar, instead. Hagar and Abram had a son called Ishmael, but rather than cheering Sarai up, it saddened her.

Abram turned ninety-nine years old and Sarai reached ninety, and still they had no

child of their own. However God insisted
that His promise remained true. "I want
you and your wife to change your names as
a sign of my vow," He said. "From now on,
you will not be Abram and Sarai, but
Abraham and Sarah. Do what I say and
trust me, and everything I have told you
will come true. You and Sarah will have
your own baby next year, you'll see. I want
you to call him Isaac."

So Abraham and Sarah continued to
wait.

Genesis chapters 11 to 13, 15 to 17

God's Promise Comes True

At long last, when Abraham was one hundred years old, Sarah had a baby boy whom they called Isaac. Everything had come to pass just as God had said.

The couple were so overjoyed that they thought nothing could spoil their happiness. But gradually, Sarah became eaten up with envy of Abraham's other son, Ishmael, whom he had with Sarah's maid, Hagar.

There had been trouble between the two women ever since Hagar had become pregnant. Because she was carrying Abraham's baby, Hagar had put on airs and graces and looked down on her mistress. Sarah had become so annoyed that she had treated Hagar badly. So badly that Hagar had eventually run away. An angel found Hagar weeping by a desert spring and comforted her, convincing her to return. God reassured Sarah too. He said that He would make Abraham and Hagar's son, Ishmael, the founder of a

39

great race. But when Abraham and Sarah had a son, Isaac, it would be his descendants who would be God's own special people.

However when Isaac was born, the rivalry Sarah felt towards Hagar brewed again. Ishmael was about fourteen and he was fond of his little brother, but Sarah hated seeing them together. She couldn't stand to be reminded that because both boys had the same father, her maid's son was equally important.

"Get rid of them!" Sarah begged Abraham. "I don't want Ishmael around, taking what should rightfully be Isaac's."

Abraham was upset because he loved both his sons. He asked God what to do.

"Don't worry," God reassured him. "Do as Sarah suggests. I'll look after Hagar and Ishmael. Trust me."

Next morning, Abraham told Hagar that she and Ishmael had to leave. With a heavy heart, he gave them food and a waterskin, and turned them out into the desert.

God kept His word and looked after Abraham's first son and his mother as they struggled to survive on their own. Once, when they were close to dying of thirst, God sent an angel to them with water. God stayed at Ishmael's side as he grew up, and he became strong and brave. Just as God had promised, He made Ishmael the founder of a great nation – the Arabs.

Genesis chapters 16, 17

A Terrible Test
for Abraham

God had put Abraham through two very difficult tests – having to journey into the unknown and having to wait for so long for he and Sarah to have a child. But Abraham's hardest test was yet to come. When their beloved son Isaac was about eleven years old, God delivered Abraham some shattering news.

"I want you to take your son to Moriah, to a place that I will show you," God told Abraham, "and offer me a sacrifice. I don't want you to kill and burn a goat or a lamb as usual, I want you to sacrifice Isaac."

Abraham was appalled. But God had spoken clearly and Abraham was quite sure what He wanted. Next morning, with agony in his heart, Abraham organized two servants to make ready to go, with firewood and provisions packed onto a donkey. Abraham told Isaac they were going on a trip, and they set off into the desert.

For two days, Abraham walked closer to the place where he was to perform the terrible deed. Then, on the third day of travelling, they came to the foot of a hill and Abraham knew it was the place God meant. "You stay here with the donkey," Abraham told the servants. "I'm going up the hill with Isaac to pray and make an offering to God."

Isaac hurried to help, unloading the donkey and lifting up the heavy bundle of wood they would need to burn the sacrifice. Abraham carried a sharp knife and a pot of red-hot coals for starting the fire.

Then the old man and his son began climbing, higher and higher, until they could no longer see the servants waiting below. At last they came to a little clearing and Abraham stopped and said in a strange, tense voice, "Here's the spot."

"Father, we've got the wood and coals to light the fire, but we've forgotten to bring an animal to sacrifice," pointed out Isaac.

Abraham couldn't bring himself to meet his son's eyes. "God will give us the animal," he said, his voice cracking with sorrow.

Then the two worked side by side to make an altar from stones and they arranged the firewood on top of it. Finally, the time had come for Abraham to do the unthinkable.

Imagine Isaac's terror when his father tied him up and lifted him onto the wood, realizing that HE was to be the sacrifice.

In anguish, Abraham raised his knife high and took a deep breath, steeling himself to kill his own son, whom he loved so much.

Just as he was about to plunge the blade downwards – "STOP!" boomed a voice from Heaven into Abraham's mind. Abraham knew it was an angel speaking. "You have proved that you love God perfectly by showing you were ready to sacrifice your son, just because He said so. That is enough

– do not harm Isaac."

Abraham dropped the knife. His shaking hands could hardly untie the rope that bound Isaac. Weeping so hard he thought his chest would burst, he held his beloved son and asked for his forgiveness.

Through his tears, Abraham caught sight of a nearby bush shaking – a ram was caught in it. "You see, Isaac. I told you that God would give us an animal for the sacrifice!" Abraham went over and caught the ram and offered it in Isaac's place.

When Abraham and his son had finished praying, they walked down the hill and returned home together.

Genesis chapter 22

A Tale of
Twin Brothers

Isaac's mother, Sarah, lived to be one hundred and twenty-seven years old, while his father, Abraham, lived to one hundred and seventy-five. By the time they both died, Isaac had married a girl called Rebecca, from Abraham's old town of Haran. Isaac inherited his father's farming business and stayed in Canaan, following God's will just as Abraham had done.

Like Isaac's father and mother, he and Rebecca had to wait a long time before God sent them children – twenty years. It was worth the wait, for when Rebecca finally found herself expecting a baby it was not one, but two – twins! A short time before they were born, God told Rebecca, "You are having two sons, who will lead two peoples. One boy will be stronger than the other and the older one will serve the younger one." At the birth, a very strange thing happened. The second baby came out holding the first one's heel, as though he wanted to pull his older brother back and overtake. Isaac and Rebecca called the elder boy Esau, because the name means 'hairy' and Esau was dark and had lots of hair. They named their younger son Jacob, which means 'someone who wants to seize somebody else's place'.

Time passed and the twins grew very different in personality as well as looks. Jacob was quiet and thoughtful. He loved spending time at home with his mother in the kitchen, and they became very close. However, Esau was strong and brave. He loved roaming around outside and he became an excellent hunter. Esau was his father's favourite son.

Whenever Jacob saw his father and brother together, talking and laughing in easy companionship, he couldn't help but wish that he was loved best by Isaac instead. To make matters worse, because Esau had been born before Jacob, the law said that Esau was to be given all of their father's wealth when he died. This was called his birthright. Jacob knew that he was cleverer than Esau and better suited to running his father's business. He couldn't stand to think that it was Esau's birthright to take it over eventually.

One day, Jacob was cooking a delicious bean stew when Esau arrived back from a hunt. "Ooooh, what's that? I'm

51

STARVING!" he exclaimed, bending over the cooking pot and breathing in the aroma. "Can I have some now?" he begged.

Jacob's eyes glinted with a sudden idea. "I'll give you some stew," he replied, "if you promise to give me all your rights as the firstborn son."

"Done!" agreed Esau. All he could think about was his rumbling stomach, burning with hunger. "If I don't get anything to eat within the next five minutes I'll fall over and die anyway, so what use would my birthright be then?" he joked.

But Jacob was quite serious. "Say you solemnly swear," he insisted.

"I solemnly swear," promised Esau. "Now come on, give me that stew!"

Jacob ladled some stew into a bowl and gave Esau some soft, baked bread, and both twins sat back, highly pleased.

Twenty years passed and Isaac was an old, blind man who knew he didn't have long to live. One of Isaac's last wishes was for Esau to go hunting for meat for his favourite meal. Afterwards, Isaac was going to give his eldest son the blessing that officially gave him his birthright. Esau gladly set off with his bow and arrows at once.

But Rebecca had overheard. All at once, a plan came to her to trick her husband into giving her favourite son Jacob the blessing instead! First, she quickly cooked the meal her husband had asked for. Then she hurriedly dressed Jacob in Esau's clothes, so he would smell like his brother, and wrapped goatskin round his arms and neck so he would feel hairy like his brother too.

"But- But- " protested Jacob.

"I'll take the blame," Rebecca reassured her son, and sent him in with the food to see his father.

The trick worked perfectly. Isaac was at first suspicious because his tasty dinner had arrived so quickly, but Jacob said that God had helped him in his hunting. Jacob copied

Esau's voice and, of course, he smelled and felt like his brother too. Isaac was fooled into thinking that Jacob was Esau, and gave him the all-important birthright blessing.

When Esau arrived back from the hunt and went to his father, they both quickly realized they had been tricked. How they wept with frustration and regret. However it was too late, the old man could not take back his blessing.

Later, in private, Esau began to feel angry. "I'll wait until father dies," he swore to himself, "but no longer than that. Then I shall have my revenge on Jacob."

Genesis chapters 25 to 28

Joseph the Dreamer

Jacob was one of the wealthiest men in Canaan. He had vast herds of cattle, sheep, goats, camels and donkeys, and he owned many tents, filled with possessions. However the thing he held most dear was Joseph, his eleventh son. Joseph's mother was Jacob's true love, Rachel. The couple had

waited for many years before God sent
them a child. So long that Jacob had
ten sons by three other wives by then. So
Joseph was very special.

Unfortunately, Jacob made it obvious
that Joseph was his favorite. He sometimes
kept Joseph at home with him while his
other sons went into the fields on
farming duties. Of course this made
Jacob's other sons resentful of their
brother. Even more so when Joseph
turned seventeen. Jacob had an
expensive coat made for him. It
was a beautiful, long coat with
big sleeves, richly sewn with
many different colors. It
drove Jacob's other sons

wild with jealousy.

The situation went from bad to worse when Joseph began to have strange dreams.

"Guess what?" he asked his brothers one morning. "Last night, I dreamt that we were in the fields at harvest time tying the wheat into sheaves, when my sheaf stood up straight. Then your sheaves gathered around it and bowed to mine!"

"Who do you think you are?" spat one of the brothers.

"Do you see yourself as better than us?" growled another.

"Do you think you're going to be a king and rule over us?" scowled a third.

A little while later, Joseph had another odd dream and again made the mistake of telling his brothers about it.

"I dreamt last night that I saw the sun, the moon and eleven stars all bowing down to me." The brothers knew that Joseph meant that their father, mother and the eleven of them were like his servants. How furious they were!

One day, when Jacob had kept Joseph at home with him and sent his other sons out to work, he decided to send Joseph to check on them. Out in the hot fields, the tired, thirsty brothers saw him coming, fresh from home, all dressed up in his fancy coat and they had a terrible idea.

"Here comes the dreamer!" one of them laughed. "I wish we could get rid of him once and for all."

"Well, this is our chance," another said.

"There's no one around, it's the perfect opportunity!" a third brother agreed.

"Let's kill him and throw the body into that pit over there," another brother urged.

"We could tell our father that he was attacked by wild animals!" one suggested.

"Stop!" cried the eldest brother, Reuben, horrified. "We can't kill Joseph! Do you really want his blood on your hands? If you must, throw him into that old, dry well over there and leave him – but don't murder him!" (Little did the brothers know that once they'd all gone home, Reuben intended to sneak back and rescue Joseph).

And that's what the brothers did. They fell on Joseph, ripping off his special coat, and then lowered him into the dried-up well, taking away the rope.

Pleased, the brothers ignored Joseph's cries for help, and sat down to eat – all except Reuben. He stomped off to see to the animals in the furthest pastures.

While Reuben was gone, a camel train of spice traders passed by on their way to Egypt. One of the brothers, Judah, had another awful idea. "Reuben was right. We shouldn't harm Joseph – he is our flesh and blood, after all," he announced, with a glint in his eye. "I have a better plan – we'll sell him instead. I'm sure the traders will pay a good price for a slave."

By the time Reuben returned, Judah and the brothers had accepted twenty pieces of silver from the traders and Joseph was gone.

"What have you done?" Reuben cried.
"Shame on you, Judah. Shame on you all!
Now what are you going to tell Father?"

In desperation, the brothers came up
with a final part to their wicked plan. They
killed a young goat, dipped Joseph's torn
coat in its blood and took it home to show
their father. "Joseph was killed and eaten by
wild animals," they explained to Jacob.

The old man collapsed in sorrow,
weeping and mourning for his beloved
Joseph. "I will grieve for my son until the
day I die," he sobbed.

Genesis chapter 37

A Slave
in Egypt

Sold by his family, marched by strangers all the way to a foreign land, and then traded in the market place as a slave – Joseph was exhausted and terrified. Yet his strong character must have shone through because the man who bought Joseph trusted him to work in his house, not in his fields or as a labourer. The man was very important and wealthy. His name was Potiphar and he was captain of the soldiers who guarded Pharaoh, the king of Egypt. God stayed with Joseph all the time and cheered him up, helping him do his duties well. Potiphar was so pleased that he kept promoting Joseph. After a while, Joseph was running Potiphar's whole household.

Now Joseph was not only hard-working and trustworthy, he was also quite handsome. So much so that Potiphar's wife fell in love with him. Each day, she seized every opportunity behind her husband's back to flirt with Joseph, trying to tempt him into having an affair. Joseph was loyal to Potiphar and kept turning her down. But

Potiphar's wife was determined to get what she wanted. One day, she lay in wait for Joseph and grabbed him by his cloak. Joseph had to wriggle out of it in order to escape her clutches and run off! Then the scorned woman saw a way to get her own back. She put on a show of being deeply upset and accused Joseph of having forced his way into her bedroom. She said that when she screamed out, he had ran away, leaving only his cloak behind.

Of course, Potiphar was furious. He had Joseph flung into prison.

Joseph could have wept and wailed. He could have despaired and died, but God stayed with him and lifted his spirits. The jailer was fond of the reliable, capable young man and began giving him special jobs. Soon, he put Joseph in charge of all the other prisoners.

Two of the prisoners in Joseph's care were Pharaoh's butler and baker. One morning, Joseph found them looking anxious because they had both had strange dreams that they couldn't understand.

"Tell me about them," Joseph urged. "Maybe God will explain to me what they're about."

"I dreamt I saw a vine on which three branches of grapes grew," said the butler. "I picked them and squeezed them into Pharaoh's cup and gave him the juice to drink."

Joseph felt sure he knew what the dream meant, thanks to God. "In three days' time Pharaoh is going to pardon you and give you your job back," he explained.

The butler was delighted. "Oh thank you! Thank you so much!" he cried.

"My friend," Joseph said, "just promise me that when you're released, you won't forget about me. Please tell Pharaoh about me and beg him to release me, for I don't deserve to be in here!"

"Well, what about my dream?" asked

the baker excitedly. "I dreamt I was carrying three baskets of white bread on my head, and the birds were eating the bread out of the top basket."

Joseph's face fell as the meaning came to him. "I hate to tell you this," he said sadly, "but in three days' time, Pharaoh is going to hang you."

The dreams came true. In three days' time, the baker was put to death, while the butler was released and set back to work for Pharaoh. He was so joyful that any thoughts of Joseph went out of his head. Joseph remained in prison, quite forgotten.

Genesis chapters 39, 40

The Ruler
of Egypt

One morning, there was a commotion in the royal palace of Egypt. Pharaoh had awoken deeply troubled. He had had two strange dreams, which he was sure meant something but he had no idea what. In the first dream, Pharaoh had been standing by the River Nile. Seven fat cows

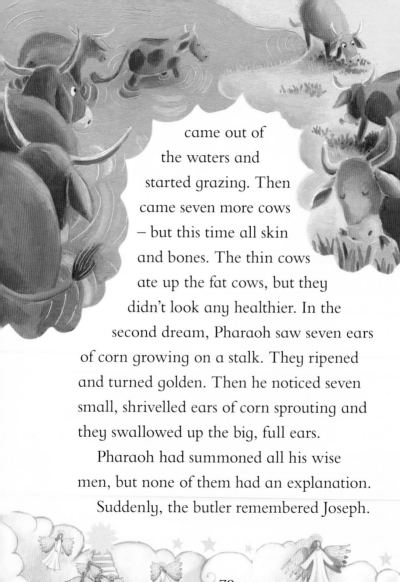

came out of
the waters and
started grazing. Then
came seven more cows
– but this time all skin
and bones. The thin cows
ate up the fat cows, but they
didn't look any healthier. In the
second dream, Pharaoh saw seven ears
of corn growing on a stalk. They ripened
and turned golden. Then he noticed seven
small, shrivelled ears of corn sprouting and
they swallowed up the big, full ears.

Pharaoh had summoned all his wise
men, but none of them had an explanation.
Suddenly, the butler remembered Joseph.

Two years had passed and he wasn't even sure if Joseph was still alive. But now he told Pharaoh all about the amazing young Israelite man locked in the dungeon.

Pharaoh sent for him at once. Joseph was hauled out of prison and brought into the magnificent courtroom of the great King of Egypt. Then Pharaoh described his dreams and Joseph felt God give him the interpretation.

"Both dreams mean the same," Joseph announced to the anxiously waiting king. "For the next seven years, Egypt will have excellent harvests. But during the following seven years the crops will fail and there will be a terrible famine. Here's what God says to do. Hire a minister with officials under him to take charge of your kingdom. For the next seven years, they should collect one-fifth of all the grain that is grown and store it away in warehouses. During the seven years of famine, you can share out the grain so your people don't starve."

"Really?" said Pharaoh. "Is that what your God thinks?" He thought for a while and everyone in the courtroom held their breath to see whether the king was pleased.

Pharaoh descended from his gleaming throne and approached Joseph. He took a huge gold ring off his finger and gave it to the former prisoner. "You will be the minister," he ordered. "I can't think of anyone better. You start straight away."

Genesis chapter 41

The Silver Cup

Joseph was now thirty years old, and Pharaoh's right-hand man. He had more power in Egypt than anyone, except the king himself.

Seven years passed. Then, as predicted, the crops failed, and not just in Egypt but in all the countries nearby. Fortunately, Joseph had made sure that the Egyptian warehouses were fully stocked. And as news of the stores spread, starving people came from far and wide to ask for food.

Among them were Joseph's brothers from Canaan. Joseph's father, Jacob, only sent ten of his sons to Egypt to buy grain. After losing Joseph he couldn't bear to part with his and Rachel's only other son, Benjamin, so he had kept him at home.

More than twenty years had passed since the brothers had sold Joseph into slavery. Joseph was now married to an Egyptian. He acted like an Egyptian. He looked like a magnificent Egyptian prince. He even spoke Egyptian. So of course, when the brothers were called into his presence to buy grain,

they didn't recognize him, but Joseph knew
who they were. He was disappointed that
Benjamin – his favourite brother – wasn't
with them, so Joseph decided to trick them
in order to get to see him.

"I don't believe you have come to ask for
grain," Joseph told his brothers through an
interpreter. "I think you are spies!"

"We're not spies, we're brothers!" they
protested. "We were twelve, but one died
long ago and the youngest of us is at home

with our father."

"Then prove it," Joseph ordered. "One of you must journey back and fetch your youngest brother. I'll give you some time to think about who is going to go." And he had them all thrown in prison.

After three days, Joseph ordered the brothers to be brought in front of him again.

"I've decided to let you return home with the grain you need," he announced. "But you must still bring me your youngest brother and to make sure you do, I shall keep one of you here as hostage."

He clapped his hands and at once, his servants grabbed Simeon, tying him up and taking him away.

It was with heavy hearts that the nine brothers set off to Canaan. They were even more dismayed when they discovered that the money they had paid for the grain was somehow in their sacks. "What's happened?" they wondered, "This is going to land us in deeper trouble." They had no idea that Joseph had ordered his servants to put the money there as another trick.

When they told Jacob that they had to return to Egypt with Benjamin, the anguished old man cried, "No! No way! I've lost Joseph, and now Simeon has gone. I'm not letting Benjamin out of my sight!"

But the weeks went by and the famine grew worse and eventually the Egyptian corn was used up. Jacob had no choice but to send his sons back to buy more – this time with Benjamin. The grief-stricken old man loaded them down with expensive gifts for the powerful Egyptian minister in the hope that he would be pleased and allow all ten of his sons to return.

As soon as Joseph heard that his brothers had arrived back in Egypt, he ordered them to be brought to the palace. The men were terrified they were going to be arrested for taking the money they had found in their sacks. "It was a mistake," they told Joseph's steward, giving it back. "Look – it's all here, count it."

But Joseph hadn't invited them to his house for that. Instead, he gave them a feast. Joseph was so delighted to see

Benjamin that he gave him five times as much to eat and drink as the others!

Next day, all ten brothers were hugely relieved to find that they were allowed to set off back to Canaan with all the grain they could carry.

However, they hadn't gone far when they heard pounding hooves behind them, and when they looked it was Joseph's steward chasing after them. He insisted on opening the brothers' sacks, from eldest to youngest, and in the last one, Benjamin's, was Joseph's best silver cup!

"Thieves!" accused the steward, knowing it was another of Joseph's tricks.

In utter despair, the brothers went with the steward back to the city and begged Joseph for forgiveness.

"Your punishment will be that Benjamin must stay here and be my slave," Joseph announced. "The rest of you are free to go."

Then Judah sprang up and pleaded, "Your Highness, our father has already lost his favourite son. If we return without this boy, he will surely die of grief. I beg you – let me stay and be your slave instead."

Then Joseph felt that his heart would break. "Everybody out!" he ordered, and his advisors left him alone with his brothers. Finally he told them who he was. "Don't blame yourselves for selling me into slavery," Joseph told the astonished men with great grace. "It was all part of God's plan for me." Then he threw his arms around Benjamin in tears, and hugged and kissed them all.

Pharaoh was delighted when he heard that Joseph had a family who were alive and well. He invited them all to live in one of the lushest parts of Egypt, where Joseph could look after them.

Jacob was reunited with his beloved son, Joseph, and lived out the last few years of his life in happiness.

Genesis chapters 41 to 46

The Baby in
the Basket

Joseph and his brothers lived in Egypt for
the rest of their lives and had many
children, grandchildren and great-
grandchildren. They did well in farming and
business and became wealthy and powerful.
As time passed, the Egyptians began calling
them Israelites after the special name God

had given to Jacob. Years went by and the number of Israelites grew, and different pharaohs came and went. After four hundred years, one king became particularly worried because there were so many Israelites. He told his advisors, "I am worried that if there was ever a war, the Israelites might turn against us and join with our enemies to defeat Egypt. We must find a way to stop their numbers growing further and to make them less powerful."

Pharaoh decided on drastic action – he sent his soldiers to seize the Israelites and turn them into slaves. Then he appointed slave-drivers to set the Israelites to work, labouring on roads and building sites, and in the fields.

But still the number of Israelites increased, and families spread further throughout Egypt. Furious, Pharaoh came up with an even more wicked plan. He ordered his soldiers to search out every newborn Israelite boy and kill them all!

Of course, many desperate families tried to hide their beloved babies. One woman, who already had a daughter, Miriam, and a son, Aaron, kept her newborn boy hidden for three months. But as time went on, he became bigger and noisier and harder to conceal. In the end, the desperate woman took a reed basket and covered it with tar so it was watertight. She gently laid her baby in it and took it down to the River Nile, setting it in the thick, tall grasses at

the water's edge so it wouldn't float away.
She told Miriam to stay a little way off to
see that the baby was alright.

It wasn't long before the little girl saw a
grand procession making its way down to
the river. Her eyes opened wide at the sight
of a young woman in magnificent robes,
splendid jewels and rich make-up,
accompanied by many servants and slaves.
It was the princess, coming to bathe! The
little girl watched, hardly daring to breathe,
as the princess caught sight of the basket in
the rushes and sent a servant to bring it to
her. As soon as the princess saw the baby
boy inside, she realized that he must be an
Israelite. As she lifted the baby up, he began
to cry and her heart melted with pity for

the hungry, helpless child. She decided to take the baby home and keep him.

Bravely, Miriam dared to approach the princess, curtseying low. "Would you like me to find an Israelite nurse to look after him, Your Highness?" she suggested nervously.

The princess was pleased, and the little girl dashed home and fetched her mother!

So the little boy was at first cared for by his real mother, then given the education of an Egyptian prince. For the princess loved him so much, she adopted him as her own son. She called him Moses, which means 'to draw out', because she had rescued him by having him drawn out of the water.

Exodus chapters 1, 2

The Burning Bush

Moses was brought up as Egyptian royalty, but he knew that he was an Israelite by birth. As he grew up, he found it unbearable that he was living a rich, comfortable life of freedom, while other Israelites suffered as Egyptian slaves. One day, when he was a young man, he saw an

Egyptian guard savagely hitting an Israelite man, and something inside him snapped. Moses beat the guard off, leaving him lying dead at his feet. News of his crime quickly spread. Moses knew that even the princess would not be able to save him from a terrible punishment, perhaps even death. He had no choice but to run away.

Moses fled to a country called Midian and settled into the quiet life of a shepherd. He looked after the flocks belonging to a village priest named Jethro, and he married his daughter, Zipporah. Years came and went and Moses' former life as an Egyptian royal seemed like a dream.

One day, Moses was out with his sheep when he came upon a very strange sight.

A bush was on fire, but the leaves and branches of the bush weren't burning away. While Moses marvelled, a voice suddenly boomed, "Moses, come no closer to this holy place! I am God – the God of your fathers, Abraham, Isaac and Jacob."

Moses fell to the ground, covering his face in terror.

"I have seen how my people, the Israelites, suffer in Egypt," echoed the voice. "But I will free them from slavery and return them to Canaan, a land of plenty that I promised would be their own. I want you to return to Egypt and rescue my people. Convince them to follow you and demand Pharaoh to release them."

Moses was shocked. "No one will believe that my orders are from you, Lord," he protested.

God gave Moses three special signs so that he could prove it. Firstly, if Moses threw his shepherd's staff onto the ground, it turned into a snake! As soon as he picked it up again, it turned back into wood. Secondly, if Moses thrust his hand into his robe, it came out covered with scales and sores of the disease leprosy! When he put it back again, it was healed and healthy.

Lastly, God told Moses that if he poured some water from the River Nile onto the ground, it would turn into blood!

Moses was stunned, but even so, he was still unsure. "How can I be a leader, Lord?" he argued. "I don't even like talking in public. I go red and can't get the words out. Isn't there someone else you can send?"

"I have already told your brother Aaron to come and find you – he can do the talking," insisted God.

Moses hurried home and explained to his wife and his father-in-law what he had been ordered to do. To Moses' great surprise, Jethro believed him. God reassured Moses that it was safe for him to return to Egypt as a new pharaoh had come to the throne.

So he and his wife packed up and set off through the countryside.

As they neared Egypt, Aaron came out to meet them, just as God had promised. The long-lost brothers hurried to see the Israelite elders straight away. While Aaron explained that God had told Moses to lead the Israelites out of slavery, Moses proved that his message was from God by demonstrating the three magic signs in front of everyone. How the Israelites gasped! They believed Moses and sent up prayers of thanks that God had sent them help.

Exodus chapters 2 to 4

The Nine
Plagues of Egypt

As God had ordered, Moses and Aaron requested an audience with Pharaoh himself. They were summoned to appear in Pharaoh's magnificent courtroom, in front of all his guards, advisors and magicians. "We have come at God's command to ask that you set the people of Israel free!" the brothers dared to tell Pharaoh.

But Pharaoh just laughed and waved for
Moses and Aaron to be taken away. Then
he set the Israelites even tougher tasks to
do, making their lives even harder and
more miserable.

"I've made the situation worse!" Moses
told God, but God insisted that he try
again.

So once more Moses and Aaron went
to see Pharaoh. This time Aaron threw
down Moses' staff, which turned into a
snake, wriggling on the floor. Pharaoh
signalled to his magicians and they too
threw their staffs onto the
floor, which
also turned

into slithering snakes. Pharaoh didn't even care when Aaron's snake swallowed up all of the magicians' snakes. "Audience over," he announced coldly.

Moses despaired, but God told him what to do. Early the next day, Moses and Aaron went down to the River Nile and waited for Pharaoh to take his morning walk there. When Pharaoh refused their demands, Aaron hit the waters with the staff. At once, the Nile turned to blood. The river ran red for seven days — all the fish died and there was no water to drink.

Yet the cold-hearted king was unmoved. Then Moses signalled Aaron to stretch the staff over the Nile, and millions of frogs came hopping out of every river, stream and pond in Egypt. Everywhere anyone looked there were frogs… anything anyone touched had frogs on it… the people couldn't move for frogs!

Then Pharaoh sent for Moses. "Tell your god to make this stop and I will let your people go."

Immediately, there were so many dead frogs that the Egyptians had to pile them into huge, stinking heaps.

Pharaoh went back on his word.

So God ordered Moses to tell Aaron to hit the ground with the staff. The dust swirled and billions of lice swarmed out of the ground and over Egypt. Soon, everything that had been slimy with leaping frogs was itching with biting lice.

But Pharaoh's heart was as hard as stone.

So God sent vast clouds of flies humming into Egypt. They darkened the skies and blanketed the ground, dive bombing people's heads, landing on their eyelids, fluttering up their nostrils. But not one fly entered the house of an Israelite.

Then Pharaoh summoned Moses. "I will do as you ask," he announced, "if your god rids us of these flies!"

Once again, as soon as the flies were gone, Pharaoh simply broke his promise.

So God sent a dreadful disease which wiped out every horse, camel, ox, goat and sheep in the land – except for those belonging to the Israelites.

Still, Pharaoh would not give in.

Then God told Moses and Aaron to take a handful of ashes and throw it up into the air. As the wind blew the ashes across Egypt, an awful sickness spread, which caused terrible boils to break out over every person and each remaining animal – unless they were Israelite.

It just made Pharaoh more determined.

So God told Moses to stretch his staff up to the heavens… Thunder crashed, lighting flashed and hail fell from the skies in mighty torrents, flattening trees and plants. Everywhere except in the fields belonging to the Israelites.

At last Pharaoh called Moses again.

"Enough!" he spat. "Make it stop and I will do what you ask." Moses prayed and the storm calmed. "I lied," announced Pharaoh triumphantly. He turned on his heel and strode away.

The very next day, a strange wind blew across Egypt, thick with locusts. Within a few hours they had eaten every blade of grass, every leaf, every ear of corn, every fruit on the trees.

"Aaaaaaargh!" howled Pharaoh. "Alright, the Israelites can go." The wind changed direction and the locusts were blown into the Red Sea and drowned.

But still, Pharaoh did not go through with his promise. So God told Moses to stretch out his hand and Egypt was swamped in total darkness for three days and nights. As his miserable people stumbled around blindly and the country ground to a halt, Pharaoh once again summoned Moses. "The Israelites may go, and this time I will not go back on my word," he spat, his eyes full of hate. "As long as they leave all their sheep, goats, camels and donkeys."

Moses listened to God.

"No," he replied, and Pharaoh turned white with fury.

"Then get out," roared the cruel king. "Your people will be my slaves forever. If I ever lay eyes on you again, you will die!"

Exodus chapters 5 to 10

The First
Passover

God spoke to Moses and said, "I am going to send one last plague upon Egypt, so terrible that Pharaoh will be glad to let the Israelites go. At midnight, every firstborn child in Egypt shall die. From the firstborn of Pharaoh to the firstborn of the lowliest servant to the firstborn of every animal. No one shall escape – unless they are an Israelite. Here's what they have to do to be spared. Every family must cook a lamb and smear their doorposts with the blood. Then I shall know which houses are Israelite homes. Forever after, this day will be called Passover and celebrated as the first day of the year. By my passing over the land tonight, my people will be set free – the beginning of a new era."

Next morning, nothing could be heard in Egypt except for wailing and screaming as people discovered their loved ones were dead. People and animals had breathed their last in every household across the land – except for the homes of the Israelites.

Once again Moses and Aaron found

themselves before Pharaoh, who was weeping over his own dead firstborn son. "Take your people and go!" he whispered. "Be gone, and never darken my lands again."

All over Pharaoh's country, the doomed Egyptians were so desperate to be rid of the Israelites that they offered them gold, silver and jewels to leave right away.

And that is how over six hundred thousand men, women and children came to walk out of Egypt. After more than four hundred years of captivity, the Israelites were heading home.

Exodus chapters 11, 12

Escape Across
the Red Sea

God Himself guided the Israelites as they travelled out of Egypt and into the wilderness beyond. By day He appeared as a column of cloud and by night, as a column of fire, so they could follow Him.

The Israelites had reached the sands of the Red Sea when they noticed a massive cloud of dust behind them in the distance, rushing towards them at great speed.

It was the Egyptian army! The minute that Pharaoh had ordered the Israelites to leave, he regretted his decision. In a whirlwind of hatred, he called for his best armour and ordered six hundred of his finest charioteers to make ready to chase after his former slaves.

The Israelites were terrified and turned on Moses. "Did you lead us out of captivity only to meet our deaths in the desert?" they cried.

"Don't be afraid," Moses told the Israelites. "The Lord will protect you, wait and see." And God spoke to Moses, telling him what to do.

With the Egyptian army thundering ever closer, Moses urged the Israelites forward – straight towards the Red Sea. Then the column of cloud blew over Pharaoh and his charioteers, smothering them so they couldn't see their way ahead. While the bewildered, frustrated Egyptians were forced to slow their pace, Moses reached the foaming seashore and stretched out his hand towards the ocean.

An immense wind blew up, nearly sweeping the Israelites off their feet. It howled and hurled, and with great gusts this way and that it split the waves. The wind drove the waters to the right and left, higher and higher, until they rolled back leaving a wide pathway of seabed in between. Then bravely and boldly, Moses strode down the sand, leading the Israelites between the towering walls of water on either side.

Then came the Egyptian army, galloping forwards. How petrified they were when they saw the waters of the Red Sea divided in front of them. Yet they plunged into the passage as the last of the Israelites reached the sandy shore on the other side.

As Pharaoh and his charioteers sped ever closer to the Israelites, Moses stretched out his hand once more. Then the towering walls of water teetered, toppled and crashed down. The Red Sea closed over the Egyptians, drowning each and every one, and the Israelites were truly free at last.

Exodus chapters 13, 14

The Ten Commandments

After three months of wandering through the hot, rocky desert, the Israelites arrived at the foot of the holy mountain of Sinai. Moses announced they would camp there a while. He told them that they should make ready with prayers and rituals because in three days' time God was going to speak to all of them.

Sure enough, on the morning of the third day, black storm clouds gathered around the peak of the mountain, hiding it from view. Thunder rumbled and lightning split the skies. Then the earth shook, and the mountain began to spew out flames and smoke as if it were an enormous furnace. A sound like a giant trumpet blared out through the air, calling the terrified Israelites to assemble at the foot of the mountain. Then Moses slowly climbed up and up towards the smoking, fiery mountain-top and disappeared from view into the clouds.

For a long time after he had gone, thunder continued to echo around the

slopes and many Israelites thought it was
the voice of God talking to their leader.
When the noise had at last died away,
Moses came back down the mountain and
announced that God had given him ten
important rules of behaviour:

1. *You must not worship any other god but me.*

2. *You must not make a statue or a picture to worship.*

3. *You must only use my name respectfully.*

4. *You must keep the seventh day, or Sabbath, of every
   week as a holy day of rest.*

5. *You must always be respectful to your parents.*

6. *You must never commit murder.*

7. *You must never be unfaithful to your partner.*

8. *You must not steal.*

9. *You must not lie.*

10. *You must not envy the things that other people have.*

Moses wrote the Ten Commandments down, and lots of other rules too. The very next day he built an altar at the foot of the mountain and asked the Israelites to vow to obey the rules. Then Moses made a sacrifice to seal their solemn promise.

Yet God still had more that He wanted the Israelites to learn, so He summoned Moses up the mountain once more, where they could talk on their own together. The Israelites watched as their leader climbed up the mountain one more time and disappeared alone into the dark clouds.

The Israelites watched and waited for Moses to return… watched and waited for seven long weeks, but there was no sign of their leader. Worried and confused, they came to the conclusion that God had abandoned them and Moses would never return.

"Make something for us to worship," they begged Aaron. "We need something we can see and touch." Thousands of men and women brought Aaron their gold jewellery. He melted it down and made an enormous statue of a calf, one of the animals that was sometimes sacrificed to God. To please the people and keep them under control, Aaron even built the calf an enormous altar and declared there would be a festival in its honour.

The people were delighted. At last they had a straightforward god. One that wasn't invisible and didn't speak to them in thunder, giving them complicated lists of things they should and shouldn't do. Immediately, the Israelites began praying to the calf and offering it sacrifices, and singing and dancing around it.

As they did so, Moses came clambering down the mountainside at last. He held two huge stone tablets on which God Himself had written out the ten most important commandments so that no one could forget them or get them wrong.

Moses knew already about how the Israelites were worshipping the golden calf because God had told him while they were up the mountain. God had been full of fury and so was Moses. Enraged at the sight that met his eyes as he approached the camp, he flung the stone tablets to the ground and they shattered into pieces. Then he hurled the golden calf into the flames of one of the sacrificial fires. "Aaron, what did everyone do to you that you allowed this to happen?" Moses was disgusted at his brother. Then he called for anyone who was on God's side to go and stand next to him. Only the men of the tribe of Levi took up places next to Moses.

On God's orders, he told each of them to grab a sword and put to death everyone who stood in their way as punishment for their sins.

Over three thousand Israelites were killed that night. The next day, Moses went back up the mountain to pray to God for forgiveness for the wickedness of His Chosen People.

Exodus chapters 19 to 24, 32

Joshua and the Battle of Jericho

The Israelites had to fight against the tribes in the lands around Canaan for many years. So many that Moses never got to enter the country that God had chosen for his people. When the time drew near that Moses realized he was going to die, he climbed up to a mountain-top and God showed him the Promised Land spread out far below. And so Moses died comforted, and a warrior called Joshua took over as ruler of the Israelites.

Then God told Joshua to be brave and bold. It was finally time to cross the River Jordan, which was all that remained to keep the Israelites from entering the Promised Land. So Joshua told the people to prepare to fight. Meanwhile, he sent spies across the river into the city of Jericho to find out what they were up against. The spies were nearly discovered by soldiers because the king of Jericho had heard that enemies had entered the city. He sent troops to search for them, but a woman called Rahab helped the spies escape. In return, she asked for their promise that Joshua's army would not harm her family when they invaded, and the spies agreed. Joshua learnt about the city and the strength of the mighty walls that surrounded it. He drew up battle plans and prayed to God for help.

Then came the day when Joshua gathered the Israelites on the banks of the River Jordan and commanded everyone to listen carefully. "As soon as the priests carrying the Ark of the Covenant step into the river, the waters will stop flowing," Joshua announced. "As long as they stand holding the Ark in the river, there will be dry land and we will all be able to cross safely to the other side."

To the Israelites' astonishment and joy, it

happened exactly as their leader had said. Finally, Joshua's army of forty thousand men stood on a plain in the Promised Land.

The walls of the mighty city of Jericho were thick and high, and the city gates were barred against them. But Joshua listened to God, who told him exactly what to do.

Every day for six days, the Israelite army marched around the city walls. Behind the soldiers, priests equipped with trumpets made of rams' horns carried the Ark of the Covenant.

For Jericho's people it was a terrifying and mysterious display of strength. What are the Israelites up to they wondered? Does that Ark really have magical powers? And

why are they marching in that eerie silence?
When will they attack?

Then on the seventh day the silence
ceased and an almighty noise began.
Joshua gave the order for the priests to blow
their horns for all they were worth as the
army marched six times around the city
walls. As they began a seventh circuit,
Joshua signalled for his soldiers to shout as
loud as they could. Then such a roaring
joined the blaring of the horns that the
walls of Jericho trembled…
and then shook… and then
with a fearful rumble,
collapsed to the ground.

Joshua's army entered
the city and killed every

man, woman and child they found there –
all except for Rahab and her household, as
she had been promised.

Deuteronomy chapter 34; Joshua chapters 1 to 6

Ruth
the Loyal

Once, there was a terrible famine around Bethlehem. A starving man called Elimelech journeyed with his wife, Naomi, and two sons to live in Moab, where things were better. Then quite suddenly Elimelech died. Naomi and her sons were grief-stricken, but they tried to

carry on as Elimelech would have wanted.
The boys married Moabite girls called Ruth
and Orpah. But then tragedy struck again
– both boys died. Naomi was heartbroken.

"I am going to return home," Naomi
told Ruth and Orpah, but Ruth refused to
see the old, lonely widow go off on her
own. "Where you go, I go," Ruth vowed.
"Your people will be my people, your god,
my god."

Naomi smiled gratefully through her
tears, and she and Ruth journeyed back to
Bethlehem together.

Ruth and Naomi were now very poor.
They struggled to make a living. One day,
Ruth was in the fields at harvest time,
collecting up the leftover corn when she

caught the eye of the farm-owner, a man called Boaz. He stopped and asked who she was. Boaz happened to be a cousin of Naomi's and he did what he could to help Ruth. Boaz told her she was welcome in his fields all the time. He told his harvesters to let her drink from their water jars whenever she wanted. He even invited Ruth to join his harvesters for a meal, giving her enough food to take home for supper. Boaz also secretly told his harvesters to leave extra corn behind so Ruth would have more to pick up.

Day after day, Boaz showed Ruth small kindnesses like these, and eventually Naomi dared to send Ruth to ask Boaz formally for his protection.

Boaz was delighted. As was tradition, he went to the city gate and declared in public that he wanted to look after Ruth and Naomi. Boaz and Ruth were married, and Boaz cared for the women all their lives.

So Ruth was rewarded for her loyalty and kindness to Naomi, and Naomi was comforted in her old age. In the fullness of time, God sent Ruth a baby boy, Obed, who brought the two women happiness. They never dreamt that Obed would have a son called Jesse, who would have a son called David, who would one day become the greatest king Israel ever had.

Ruth chapters 1 to 4

David and
the Giant

The people of Israel saw that other
nations had kings to rule them and
demanded that they should have one too.
The great prophet Samuel asked God for
approval. He was told to choose a man
called Saul from the tribe of Benjamin to be
the first king of Israel.

King Saul won many victories against Israel's enemies, but he did not always do as God wanted. For this reason, God told Samuel that Saul's sons would never be king. God ordered that Samuel travel to Bethlehem and find a shepherd boy called David, the youngest son of a man called Jesse. It was David that God wanted to be the next king. Samuel did so, and gave David a special blessing, and from then on God was always with him.

King Saul's army often had to fight the Philistines because they were constantly invading Israelite territory. Every Israelite who could be spared was called to defend their lands, and three of Jesse's other sons went to the frontline. One day, Jesse sent

David off with food supplies for them. He reached the camp as a battle was beginning and the armoured soldiers were marching onto the battlefield. Suddenly, they all turned and came running back in fear.

"Whatever is going on?" David called as one terrified soldier ran past.

The man just shouted, "Look!" and pointed behind him.

Striding out in front of the Philistine army was a warrior more enormous than David could have dreamt. He was almost twice as big as everyone else!

"Run away if you like," the giant bellowed.

"There's no need to do battle if you're too cowardly. Just send someone to fight me in single combat. Whoever wins has victory for their side. Now, is any one of you men big enough to take up the challenge?" He smashed his mighty spear against his shield and threw back his head and roared, and the noise crashed around the surrounding hills like thunder.

David was outraged. "How dare he! It's an insult not just to us but to God!" he spat. "Just let me at him! Out in the pastures, I've killed lions and bears when they've attacked my father's flocks and I can do the same to this beast too! God protected me then as He will protect me now."

"Well…" said Saul, casting around for

other volunteers. None were forthcoming. "Very well, and God be with you." Saul insisted on dressing David in his own armour, but it was so big and bulky that he couldn't move, so David took it off again. He strode out to meet the giant, Goliath of Gath, with just his staff, his slingshot and five smooth stones in his shepherd's pouch.

King Saul and his army watched in amazement. The giant was roaring with laughter as a mere child walked towards him. The young boy was yelling back that he was going to slay Goliath in the name of God. The shepherd boy stood firm as the giant ran towards him with death in his eyes, brandishing his spear. Then David raised his slingshot and whirled it around

once… A stone struck Goliath in the
forehead, sending him crashing to the
ground, dead. As King Saul and his army
cheered, David drew
the giant's sword and
cut off Goliath's head
with one blow.
And the Philistines
turned and fled, leaving the
Israelites triumphant.

I Samuel chapters 8, 9, 16, 17

Solomon
the Wise

When Saul, the first king of Israel
died, David came to the throne,
just as God had wanted. It was King David
who made Israel a great, unified nation
with Jerusalem as its capital city. He had
the Ark of the Covenant brought there amid
great rejoicing. He wanted to build a

glorious temple to house it, but God told
David that He was going to entrust that job
to his son, Solomon, the third king of Israel.

Solomon was in his early twenties when
he took over the throne. He was determined
to carry on his father's good work,
strengthening the nation and keeping peace
with Israel's enemies, but he wasn't sure
exactly how to do it. He felt he lacked the
experience and confidence he needed to be
a good king.

One night, God appeared to Solomon in
a dream and asked how He could help.
"Please, God, give me the gift of wisdom,"
the king begged.

God was delighted. Solomon could have
asked for gold or a long life or power over

his enemies, or a whole range of other selfish things. Wisdom to govern the people well was an excellent choice and God was only too happy to oblige.

Not long afterwards, two women who were in the middle of a bitter argument were brought before Solomon so he could settle their dispute. The women lived together and both had recently given birth to a child. However, one of the babies had died, and now each woman was claiming the living baby as hers.

"It's her baby who died," the first one insisted to Solomon. "Do you think I don't know my own child?"

"No, her baby died!" the second woman protested. "Then she stole mine."

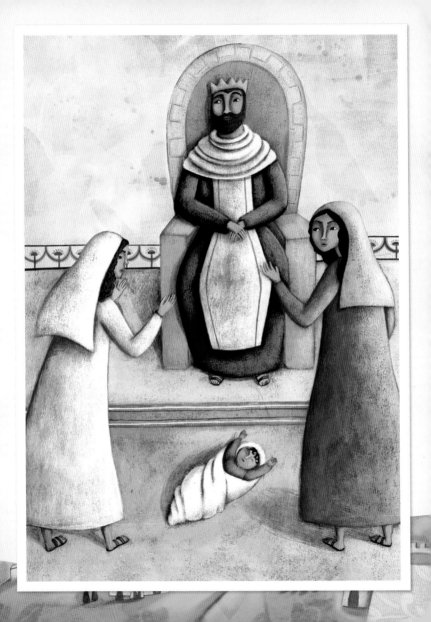

Solomon signalled for the women to be quiet. After a few minutes he announced, "Bring me my sword!" As the weapon was fetched he continued, "Cut the child in two and give half to each woman!"

"Yes, neither of us should have him!" cried one woman.

But the other burst out wailing. "Sire, please! I would rather see him given away to her than for him to be hurt!"

Then Solomon knew who the real mother of the baby was. And all the people of Israel knew that such wisdom could only have come from God.

II Samuel chapters 5 to 7; I Kings chapters 1, 3

Jonah and
the Giant Fish

One day, God told a man called Jonah,
"Go to Assyria, to the capital city of
Nineveh. Tell the wicked people there about
me and make sure they change their sinful
ways."

Now Jonah didn't care for these people
and wasn't much bothered if they found out

about God or not. He also didn't like the sound of walking into the capital city of a powerful, war-like nation and telling the people what they were doing wrong. So Jonah got on a boat in the opposite direction to Nineveh, heading for Spain.

As soon as the ship was on its way, God sent a mighty storm its way. The sailors were terrified and began praying to be saved. Still the rain lashed the boat and the wind and waves hurled it this way and that. Then the sailors decided that someone on board must be cursed. They drew lots and came up with Jonah's name.

Shamefully, Jonah confessed that he was disobeying God by being on the boat. "You'll have to throw me overboard," he wept, "it's the only way you'll get this storm to stop." The sailors were horrified and did their best to row to shore. But when the storm grew even worse they concluded there was only one thing for it – and dropped Jonah into the water.

The minute they did so, the wind dropped, the rain stopped, the waves died away, and the ship was saved. God saved Jonah too. Instead of letting him sink and drown, He sent a massive fish that swallowed him. For three days Jonah wallowed in the stinky darkness of the fish's belly, praying to God for another chance. Finally, to his relief, the fish spat him out onto a sandy shore.

"Go to Nineveh," God said again, "and give the people my message. If they don't change their behaviour, I will destroy the city after forty days."

This time Jonah did what he was told. To his immense surprise the Assyrians listened. The king of Nineveh believed God's threat and ordered his people to mend their ways. Soon, there was a drop in crime. People started being more polite and kind to each other. They prayed for forgiveness and fasted, and started worshipping God. The forty days came and went and God left the city and its people untouched.

Jonah stomped off on his own into the countryside. "I knew this would happen!" he moaned to God, sitting down in protest. "I've come all this way – nearly drowned, been eaten by a fish, then walked for miles to face crowds of hostile strangers – and all for nothing. You haven't punished anyone or destroyed anything at all."

God decided to teach the angry man a lesson. He made a tree shoot up swiftly right where Jonah was sitting, so all day he could rest in its cool shade. However the next day, God sent insects to eat the tree so it shrivelled and died, leaving Jonah sitting in the blazing sun. God also sent desert wind to roast him. "If only my poor tree hadn't died!" Jonah groaned.

"Well," said God kindly, "if you're upset about a tree – a tree that you neither planted nor looked after – how upset do you think I would have been if the city of Nineveh had been lost? One hundred and twenty thousand people live there, not to mention all the animals."

And Jonah finally understood that God cared for all people, not just the Israelites – and for animals too. After all, hadn't God made them in the first place?

Jonah

Daniel in the Lions' Den

Daniel was such an outstanding advisor that King Darius of the Medes and Persians put him in charge of his whole empire. The other officials were so jealous that they came up with an idea that was certain to land Daniel in trouble. They suggested to Darius that he should order that no one pray to anyone but him for thirty days. If anyone disobeyed, they were to be thrown into a pit of hungry lions. The king thought it was a great idea and signed the order.

Now Daniel was a good, holy man. Of course, he continued to pray to God three times a day, as always in front of his window in full view of passers-by.

It wasn't long before his enemies reported him to the king. Darius was devastated, but he could not go back on his word. He ordered that Daniel should be thrown to the lions. "May your god save you," the king prayed, and a huge stone was placed over the pit so there was no way Daniel could escape.

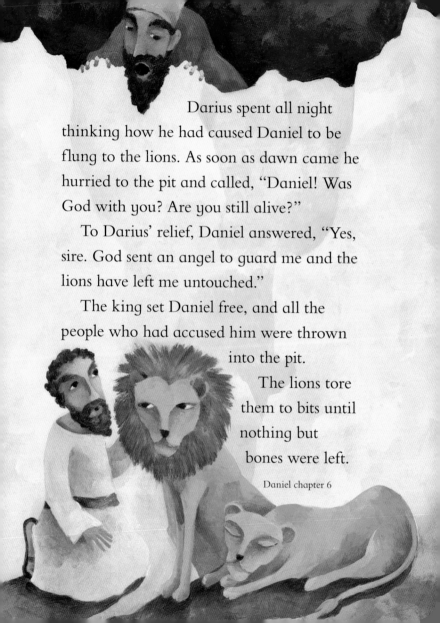

Darius spent all night thinking how he had caused Daniel to be flung to the lions. As soon as dawn came he hurried to the pit and called, "Daniel! Was God with you? Are you still alive?"

To Darius' relief, Daniel answered, "Yes, sire. God sent an angel to guard me and the lions have left me untouched."

The king set Daniel free, and all the people who had accused him were thrown into the pit.

The lions tore them to bits until nothing but bones were left.

Daniel chapter 6

THE NEW TESTAMENT

The New Testament is the name for the second section of the Bible, made up of twenty-seven books. It describes the birth, life and death of a man called Jesus, His teachings about God and His followers. Jesus lived two thousand years ago in the Middle East. At that time, the Romans controlled these lands and the Jewish people who lived there were unhappy about it. They were waiting for a saviour – the 'Messiah' – who would establish a mighty kingdom for them. The New Testament was written by the followers of Jesus, who believed Him to be the Messiah, during the one hundred years after He died.

The Angel Gabriel Brings News 150
His Name is John 155
The Birth of Jesus 158
The Shepherds' Visit 165
Follow the Star 170
Flight from Danger 176
Jesus in the Temple 179
John the Baptist 184
Jesus is Tempted 189
Jesus' First Miracle 194
Jesus Goes Fishing 198
Jesus Chooses Special Helpers 202

Jesus the Healer. 205
Jesus Befriends Outcasts. 209
Jesus Calms the Storm. 214
Two Fish and Five Loaves. 217
Walking on Water. 222
A Visit to Martha and Mary. 228
Lazarus is Awoken 233
Jesus Teaches through Stories 238
The Good Samaritan 242
A Story of Forgiveness. 248
Jesus and the Children 254
Jesus the Good Shepherd 258
Jesus Warns of the Future 261
The First Palm Sunday 265
Jesus and the Temple Traders 270
Jesus Against the Authorities 273
The Last Supper. 277
The Garden of Gethsemane. 283
Jesus on Trial 289
The Crucifixion. 295
The First Easter 301
Jesus and Doubting Thomas 307
The Stranger on the Beach. 311
The Ascension into Heaven. 314
The Coming of the Holy Spirit. 317

The Angel Gabriel
Brings News

There once lived in Galilee an old priest called Zachariah and his wife Elisabeth. Both were good Jewish people who always tried to live by God's rules. However, they were sad because they had never been able to have children.

One day Zachariah was given a special

honour. It was his turn to go into the great temple in Jerusalem, to the most sacred altar, and make an offering to God. As he did so, deep in prayer, an angel suddenly appeared. Zachariah was terrified.

"Don't be afraid," the angel said. "I have come with great news. God is going to answer the prayers of you and your wife, begging for children. He is going to give you a son. God wants you to call him John. Your son is going to be a very holy man and will do great work for Him."

Zachariah was stunned. Was he really seeing and hearing an angel? And even if he was, Elisabeth was past the usual age for having children. "Are you sure?" he asked in disbelief. "How can this be?"

"I am Gabriel,
a messenger
from God!"
the angel
said sternly.
"Because you
haven't believed me
you will stay silent until it
comes true!" And the angel
disappeared, just as suddenly as
he had arrived.

Imagine Elisabeth's surprise when her
husband came home unable to speak. He
had to explain what had happened by
acting things out and writing things down.
Imagine Elisabeth's amazement when a
short while later her husband's prediction

came true and she found that she was pregnant. Elisabeth was astonished when six months later, her younger cousin Mary arrived unannounced. All at once Elisabeth knew that Mary was also having a baby – a very special baby indeed.

Just as mysteriously, Mary knew about Elisabeth's baby. Bursting with excitement and happiness, she explained everything to her cousin. Mary had been going about her chores one day as usual when suddenly the angel Gabriel appeared in her little home in the town of Nazareth. It was he who had told her that Elisabeth was going to have a baby. But the angel had even more important news for Mary. Gabriel told her that God thought she was very special and that He was going to make her the mother of His son. Mary was going to have a little boy, and God wanted Mary to call him Jesus. "He will be ruler over all the Lord's people and His Kingdom will have no end," the angel told the stunned woman.

Mary hurried off to visit Elisabeth straight away so she could share her joy with her cousin. She stayed as long as she could to help the older lady through her pregnancy. But before Elisabeth's baby was born, Mary had to return home to prepare for the birth of her own child.

Luke chapter 1

His Name is John

The day came when Elisabeth gave
birth to a baby boy just as the angel
Gabriel had said. Her neighbours and
relatives came to admire the new arrival.
Everyone marvelled at what a miracle it
was that Elisabeth had been able to have a
baby at her age.

When the baby was one week old, the family held a party to promise him to God and to officially name him. Everyone assumed that the couple were going to call the boy Zachariah because it was tradition for the first son to be named after his father. Elisabeth caused a stir when she announced that the baby was to be named John.

"John!" Elisabeth's relations exclaimed. "There's no one in our family called John. Where on earth have you come up with that name from?" Turning to Zachariah, they asked, "Zachariah, you want your son to be named after you, don't you? Of course you do! Tell Elisabeth immediately."

Poor Zachariah still couldn't speak. Very frustrated, he signalled around for

something to write with. Someone hurried
to find him a writing tablet. Then
Zachariah wrote the biggest, boldest letters
he could fit on the tablet
and then held it up so
everyone could see. It read:
HIS NAME IS JOHN.

Everyone grumbled,
but in the midst of their
murmurings Zachariah suddenly
found he could speak again. "My voice has
come back!" he cried. "Thank you, God,
for everything you have done for us!"

It wasn't long before the news of what
had happened at the party had spread far
and wide.

Luke chapter 1

The Birth
of Jesus

Mary was engaged to marry a young man called Joseph, a local carpenter. When she told Joseph she was expecting a baby he was very upset. The baby couldn't be his because they weren't married. And in those days, if an unmarried woman was expecting a baby it was quite shameful.

However, Joseph had a dream in which an angel told him, "Don't be afraid to take Mary as your wife. Her baby is the Son of God Himself. The prophets of long ago foretold that He would come and save everyone from their sins. Raise Him as your own son. God wants you to call Him Jesus." After this Joseph felt much better. He realized he would be honoured to bring the little boy up as his own, and he and Mary were married straight away.

However, near the time that the baby was to be born, another problem arose. The emperor Augustus Caesar ordered a survey of all the people in his lands. He commanded that every man had to travel to where he was born, taking his family with him to have their names put on a register. Joseph had been born in the city of Bethlehem in Judea, in the south of the country, which was quite a distance from the village of Nazareth. Mary was heavily pregnant and travelling would be very difficult for her. Nevertheless, the couple did not have a choice. They packed what they would need for the trip and set off. Mary couldn't possibly walk all that way, so she rode on a donkey. It was a bumpy and tiring journey for a woman so close to having a baby.

By the time the couple

reached Bethlehem they were exhausted, hungry and dusty. Joseph began trying to find a room in which they could stay. He trudged with the donkey and Mary from one lodging place to the next. But to the couple's dismay, everywhere was full. The city was bustling with travellers who had come to register for the emperor's survey.

As they were turned away from one place after another, Mary began to feel that the baby was on its way. Hurriedly, Joseph banged on the door of the nearest inn. After a few moments, the busy innkeeper peered outside. "Don't bother asking, we're full," he said, as soon as he saw the travellers.

"Wait, please help us!" cried Joseph, stopping the innkeeper from shutting the door on them. "My wife's about to have a baby. She can't give birth out here in the street! Haven't you got a spare corner somewhere you could squeeze us in?"

"Well..." said the innkeeper, looking at poor Mary in pain on the donkey. "I haven't got a single room to spare, but you're welcome to shelter in my stable if you don't mind the animals."

"Thank you, thank you so much," Joseph said, gratefully shaking the man's hand, and the innkeeper showed them the way to his stable.

It was there, with the donkeys, oxen and sheep looking on, that Mary gave birth to the baby boy who was to be the saviour of the world. She wrapped Him up in cloths

and nestled Him in a manger full of straw.
And baby Jesus was warm and safe, with
His mother and foster father by His side.

Matthew chapter 1; Luke chapter 2

The Shepherds' Visit

On the night that Jesus was born, the city of Bethlehem throbbed with people, while the surrounding countryside was peaceful except for a few shepherds and their flocks. The shepherds were taking turns at sleeping and watching. They made sure that the sheep weren't wandering away and kept watch for hungry wolves.

All at once the starry night sky above the shepherds blazed as bright as day. Then it blazed brighter still, too bright for the shepherds to look up. They shielded their eyes from the blinding glare as an angel appeared high overhead. The shepherds were terrified.

"Don't be afraid," came the angel's voice, clear through the still, cold night. "I bring you wonderful news – wonderful news for everyone on Earth. This very night a child has been born who will be the saviour of all people. You can find Him in a stable in Bethlehem, lying in a manger."

The air was filled with singing more beautiful than the shepherds had ever heard, as hundreds of thousands of angels suddenly appeared in the heavens.

"Glory to God," they sang. "And peace to all people on Earth."

The shepherds stood transfixed until the angels had finished their song. Then the heavenly music died and the angels faded away.

Could it really be true the shepherds wondered? In ancient stories prophets had predicted for hundreds of years that a man would come who would save everyone from

their sins. They called him the Messiah.
Maybe he had really come at last.

The shepherds hurried off to Bethlehem,
to see for themselves. They searched
through the streets until they heard the
sound of a newborn baby crying from a
stable behind an inn. There they found
Mary and Joseph looking after baby Jesus.
In great excitement, they told the startled
couple all that they had seen and heard.
Mary fell very quiet, taking it all in.

The shepherds stayed for a while,
marvelling at the baby boy who they had
been told was the Messiah, but they had to
return to their flocks. All the way back they
couldn't stop talking about the amazing
chorus of angels and how their words had

come true. They told everyone they met, praising God and giving thanks for all that they had seen and been told.

Luke chapter 2

Follow
the Star

Far away in distant lands to the east,
there lived some wise men who were
astrologers. Every night they gazed up at
the sky and studied the stars, trying to work
out what their movements around the
heavens meant for people on Earth. One
night they were stunned by a brand new

star that appeared much
bigger and brighter than the
rest. They hurried to consult their
ancient books to see what it could
mean. The wise men became very
excited by what they found, and were in
no doubt that a great Jewish prophecy had
come true. The star was a sign that a baby
had been born who would become the king
of God's Chosen People. The wise men
decided to set off to find him at once. They
packed up their camels with supplies and set
off into the desert, heading in the direction
of the star that blazed each night in the sky.
They arrived in the city of Jerusalem.

News soon reached King Herod of Judea
that strangers from the east had arrived in

Jerusalem. These strangers were searching
for a newborn baby they were calling the
'King of the Jews'. Of course Herod didn't
like the sound of that at all. As far as he was
concerned he had been crowned King of
the Jews and he wanted it to stay that way.
He certainly wasn't going to put up with
rumours spreading about a rival – who
fulfilled one of the ancient prophecies no
less. It would just stir up trouble among the
people and they might rise up against him.

King Herod set about dealing with the
problem in his cold, calculated way. First, he
called a meeting of all the chief Jewish
religious leaders to find out more. "Where
do your ancient books say the Messiah is to
be born?" he asked, innocently.

"In Bethlehem," the holy men answered.

Then King Herod called his guards and ordered them to find the wise men and bring them to him. "But do it in secret," he commanded. "I don't want people to get the impression that I think these men and their rumours are important."

The wise men were nervous when they were summoned to see the king. They had heard that Herod could be a cruel leader. However, they were surprised to find him most polite, interested and even helpful in their quest. "The Jewish elders have told me that you shouldn't be looking in Jerusalem," he explained. "Try Bethlehem instead. When you have found the future king, do come back and tell me all about it.

I'd like to go and pay my respects too."

The wise men had no idea that King Herod only wanted to know where the baby was so he could have him killed.

They set off to Bethlehem and followed the star to where it appeared to hang biggest and brightest in the sky, over the house in which Mary and Joseph were now staying. The wise men were surprised to find the baby in an ordinary home rather than a splendid palace. They bowed to worship Him and presented Mary and Joseph with gifts – jewelled gold caskets, and the rare spices frankincense and myrrh.

Herod never got to hear of the wise men's success. The night before they were due to set off home, they had a troubling dream that warned them not to return to the king. The wise men took a different route back to their lands in the east and Herod never found them.

Matthew chapter 2

Flight from Danger

After the wise men had visited Jesus, an angel appeared to Joseph in a dream. "Herod is trying to find the baby to kill Him," the angel warned. "Take Him and Mary to Egypt. It will be a long, hard journey, but it will take you safely out of the cruel king's reach. Stay there until I tell

176

you it is safe to return."

Joseph woke up with a start. He woke
Mary and told her to make ready to travel
straight away. The family hurried through
the dark, sleeping streets of Bethlehem
and onto the road to Egypt.

Meanwhile back in Jerusalem,
Herod was waiting for the wise
men to return from Bethlehem
and tell him where the baby king
of kings was. He waited… and
waited… Eventually he realized
that the wise men weren't
coming – he had been tricked!
Herod flew into a fury and roared
at his army chief, "Send your men
to search every house in Bethlehem.

I want every boy under two years of age put to death immediately!"

By the time the soldiers arrived in Bethlehem to carry out their terrible task, Jesus, Mary and Joseph were miles away in Egypt. They stayed there for several months until an angel appeared to Joseph once more, telling him that King Herod had died and it was safe to go back to Israel. However Joseph did not take his family back to Bethlehem. The city was far too close to Jerusalem, where King Herod's son was now on the throne. Instead, he travelled north back to their home in the sleepy town of Nazareth in the remote area of Galilee.

Matthew chapter 2

Jesus in
the Temple

Every year at the festival of Passover, all
Jewish men went to visit the temple in
Jerusalem, to pray and give thanks to God.
Joseph always went and, like many women,
Mary went too. Of course the number of
people who crowded into the city was huge.
The lodging houses were heaving, people

packed streets and the temple itself was totally crammed. Like many parents with young children, Mary and Joseph left Jesus with a relative or neighbour when they went to celebrate the festival. But when He reached the age of twelve, they decided Jesus was old enough to go with them.

The family travelled to Jerusalem with a large group of relatives and friends. When the festival was over, they all set off to travel home. Joseph walked with the men, Mary chatted to the women and Jesus ran back and forth with the other children.

But at the end of the first day's journey, when the group of travellers began to make camp for the night, Jesus had disappeared. Mary and Joseph called for their son at the

tops of their voices, but He didn't come.
With a rising sense of panic, the couple
dashed up and down, describing Jesus to
everyone and asking if anyone had seen
Him. No one had. Darkness was drawing
in fast. "There's nothing else we can do
tonight, but as soon as it gets light
tomorrow we'll retrace our steps and find
Him," Joseph comforted his weeping wife.

Of course, Mary and Joseph didn't sleep
for worrying about where Jesus was and
whether He was safe. At sunrise Mary and
Joseph began making their way back to
Jerusalem, asking everyone they met if they
had seen a lost twelve-year-old boy. They
reached the city and hunted around its
bustling streets for two days, but there was

no sign of Him.

The third day came and in desperation Mary and Joseph went to look in the great temple itself. To their astonishment, there they found Jesus deep in discussion with a group of Jewish priests and leaders.

"Your son has such a wise understanding of the ancient writings, we can't believe He is only twelve," the holy men told Mary and Joseph. "He asks questions that most people never think to ask, and He's been giving us answers too!"

But Mary and Joseph just wanted to know what had happened to Jesus. "Where on earth have you been?" They cried. "We've been worried sick!"

Jesus replied calmly, "You should have known that you would find me in my Father's house."

Luke chapter 2

John the Baptist

Elisabeth and Zachariah's son John grew up to be a holy man. He went to live on his own in the countryside of Judea, so he could think about God and pray without being distracted. He wore only a simple robe woven from camel hair and survived by eating locusts and wild honey. When he was about thirty years old, he began preaching to anyone he came across. "Be sorry for your sins and turn away from evil," was his message, "so you can enter God's Kingdom, which is nearly here!"

John was such a powerful speaker that people travelled especially to see him. People from all walks of life flocked from towns, villages and the city of Jerusalem too. From poor common people, to powerful Jewish groups such as the Pharisees and the Sadducees, as well as farmers, shop-keepers, tax collectors and even Roman soldiers. They usually found John on the banks of the River Jordan.

"What does God want from us?" they would ask.

John would advise, "Be kind and generous. Treat each other fairly. Don't hurt anyone, neither in your actions nor words."

John's teachings were so stirring that people often asked him if he was the saviour – the Messiah spoken of in the ancient writings. "No," John would insist, "but I am trying to prepare the way for His coming."

One after the other, people would tell John all the things they had done wrong in their lives, hanging their heads in shame. They felt truly sorry for their sins and promised they wouldn't do them again, and that they would turn to God and try to live by His rules. Then John baptized them in the holy river. He dipped the people into the water and gave them God's blessing, so their sins were washed away and they could begin afresh. "I'm only baptizing you with water," John told them, "but the man who is coming will baptize you with the fire of the Holy Spirit. He is so holy that I am not even good enough to undo his sandals."

One day, among the crowd on the banks of the Jordan, Jesus was waiting to be baptized. John knew who He was immediately. "It's not right that I baptize you," John told Jesus. "You should be baptizing me."

But Jesus insisted that it was what God wanted. So together the men walked into the river. As soon as John had baptized Jesus, the clouds above them parted and

light blazed down on Jesus. A dove came
gliding down and hovered above Jesus, and
John knew that it was God's Holy Spirit
coming down to Him. Then a voice spoke
into everyone's minds saying, "This is my
beloved son, with whom I am very pleased."

Matthew chapter 3; Mark chapter 1; Luke chapter 3; John chapter 1

Jesus is Tempted

Jesus went into the desert lands of Judea so He could think undisturbed about God and what He wanted Him to do. Jesus was all alone except for the wild animals. He prayed for forty days and forty nights, until He was weak with tiredness and hunger. Then the devil came to Jesus in His thoughts, trying to tempt Him into committing a sin.

"If you really are the Son of God," said the devil, "turn these stones into bread."

But Jesus refused to do so. He had heard God call Him His son when John baptized Him. He didn't need to work a miracle to prove it, and He knew it would be wrong to do so just to make life easier. Even though Jesus felt like fainting through hunger, He trusted God to look after him.

The devil was angry, and he tried again. He made Jesus feel as though He was standing on the roof of the great temple in Jerusalem, looking down on the bustling courtyards below. "Announce to everyone that you are the Son of God," the devil

said, "then throw yourself off. The angels
will surely catch you!"

But Jesus refused to do so again. He
knew it would be wrong to test God in this
way. And God wanted to win followers
because people loved Him, not just because
they'd seen a miracle.

The devil was bursting with fury but he
refused to give up. He tried for a third time
to get Jesus to sin. The devil made Jesus feel
as if He was standing on top of a very high
mountain. When He looked down He could
see all the countries of the world spread out
beneath Him.

"Look," whispered the devil in Jesus' ear.
"This is what I can give you – all the lands
and peoples from one end of the Earth to

the other – if you will just bow down and
worship me."

Jesus knew that a lot of people
had turned to wickedness in order to
make themselves powerful rulers.
But the kingdoms the devil
helped them establish were
full of cruelty and misery.
Moreover, Jesus knew that
only one kingdom would
last forever – the
Kingdom of God.

"No! Get away from me!" roared Jesus. "I will only worship God."

The devil was defeated and he crept away. As Jesus sank down, utterly exhausted, angels came to look after Him.

Matthew chapter 4; Mark chapter 1; Luke chapter 4

Jesus' First Miracle

Jesus left the River Jordan and the desert lands of Judea in the south behind Him and went back to live in Galilee in the north. He knew God wanted Him to begin teaching everyone what they had to do to enter His Kingdom. Several followers of John the Baptist went with Jesus to help.

Jesus preached in Jewish places of worship called synagogues. "Beg God to forgive your sins," He told everyone, just like John the Baptist had, "so you can enter the Kingdom of God, which is coming." News soon spread that Jesus was an exciting speaker and He quickly built a following.

Not long after Jesus had arrived back in Galilee, His mother Mary told Him that they had been invited to a wedding in Cana. It was to be a big event and the wedding celebrations were set to go on for several days.

Sitting down at the feast for the wedding everyone was having a wonderful time. About halfway through, Mary noticed that the wine was starting to run out. She knew

it would be highly embarrassing for the
bride and bridegroom if they couldn't offer
their guests any more to drink. So she
whispered to Jesus, feeling sure that He
could help.

"I'm sorry but I can't do anything about
it," Jesus whispered back. "It's not a good
time right now."

But Mary turned to the flustered servants
and said, "I've noticed that you are low on
wine, but my son can help. Do exactly what
He says."

Jesus sighed. He gave his mother a gentle
smile. Then He told the servants, "Fill all the
empty wine jars up to the brim with water."
They hurried to do as He said. "Now pour
some into a goblet and take it to your boss,

the steward, for tasting," Jesus instructed. They did so, rather worried, but to their astonishment the steward smacked his lips, clapped his hands and ordered it to be served to the guests at once. The water had turned into wine. Not only that, but excellent wine – better than they had previously been serving. The steward strode straight over to the bridegroom to congratulate him on his good taste and generosity.

Through the power of God His Father, Jesus had performed His first miracle. There were many more to come.

Matthew chapter 4; Mark chapter 1; Luke chapter 4; John chapters 1, 2

Jesus Goes Fishing

Jesus sailed out on the Sea of Galilee in a boat belonging to two of His followers, Peter and Andrew who were fishermen. "Throw your nets into the water. Let's see if there are any fish today," Jesus suggested.

"We already know there aren't," Peter replied gloomily. "We were fishing all last night and we didn't catch a thing."

"Well, why not try again?" Jesus urged.

"I don't think there's much point," Peter shrugged. Then he saw a strange gleam in Jesus' eyes. "But I suppose there's no harm in having another go."

He and Andrew lowered their nets and waited… Then after a while, the brothers went to lift them up again. To their astonishment, the nets were so heavy with fish that they couldn't raise them. The stunned pair had to signal for help from a nearby boat, belonging to the two sons of a man called Zebedee. Their names were James and John and they rowed over to help.

Jesus watched the four men work hard together. It took all their strength to heave

the enormous catch aboard. Soon Peter's
and Andrew's little boat was full of shiny,
wriggling fish, and so weighed down in the
water that it was in danger of sinking.

The men knew that this sort of catch was unheard of. Something miraculous must have happened. Peter fell on his knees before Jesus and said, "Lord, I'm not good enough to be one of your followers. I shouldn't have doubted what you said, I should have just done it straight away."

"Don't worry," Jesus said, kindly. "Anyway, I'm going to show you how to catch people instead of fish…"

From then on, Peter, Andrew, James and John stayed at Jesus' side and helped him.

Matthew chapter 4; Mark chapter 1; Luke chapter 5

Jesus Chooses Special Helpers

Jesus became so well known that He couldn't go anywhere without being surrounded by crowds. He once climbed high up a mountain so He could be on His own. Jesus prayed to God all night. When He came down the

next day, He summoned twelve men from
His many disciples.

They were brothers Peter and Andrew,
brothers James and John, a former follower
of John the Baptist called Philip, Matthew
the tax collector, a man called Simon who
was a member of a Jewish group called the
Zealots, a second James, and four others –
Thomas, Bartholomew, Thaddaeus
and Judas Iscariot.

Jesus took the twelve men to one side
and spoke to them. "I want you to be
my special helpers," He explained. "I
want each of you to go and preach to
people what I have preached. I am
going to give you the power to heal
the sick, just as I do. Don't accept any

money for it. Don't take anything on your travels except for the clothes you are wearing, just live off people's kindness. It won't be easy – some people will ignore you, others will try to stop you spreading my message and some may even try to have you killed. But God will always be with you, looking after you, and His Holy Spirit will give you courage. And if you give up your life for me, I promise you will have a new and happier life in Heaven."

So for several weeks, the twelve men went out around the countryside, teaching and healing in Jesus' name.

Matthew chapter 10; Mark chapters 3, 6; Luke chapters 6, 9

Jesus
the Healer

Soon people from far and wide came to
hear about Jesus. Men, women and
children were excited by the sound of this
captivating preacher who worked miracles.
They began seeking Jesus out, travelling to
wherever He was to see Him for themselves.
Jesus tried to help as many people as He

could and convince them to turn to God.

After Jesus had preached in one place, a man who was suffering from the terrible skin disease leprosy crept up to Him. He was extremely nervous about approaching Jesus. Leprosy was very contagious and also incurable, and most people didn't want lepers anywhere near them. In fact, people usually ran away when they saw a leper coming. But Jesus didn't. The poor man knelt before Him, his skin misshapen and ugly with sores, and said, "I know that you can cure me, if you want to."

"Of course I want to," Jesus murmured, and He reached out and placed His hand on the leper's crumbling skin.

It took a couple of moments for the leper

to recover from the shock. After all, most people wouldn't dream of touching him.

But then the man looked at his hands, his legs and felt his face. His skin was healed. He was cured!

"Don't tell anyone," Jesus told the man, who was sobbing his gratitude. "Just go to your priest so he can see for himself and make an offering of thanks to God."

Another time, Jesus shocked many people when He helped an officer in the Roman army. After all, most Jewish people hated the Romans because they had taken control of Israel. The Roman officer begged Jesus to help his servant who was lying ill at home in great pain. "I will come with you straight away," Jesus told the Roman officer.

"That won't be necessary," the Roman insisted. "I know if you just give the word for my servant to recover, he will do so."

Jesus was stunned and delighted. "I haven't met a Jewish person who has shown as much faith as this," He said. "There will be many people from far-off lands who will be able to enter the Kingdom of Heaven, while many from the nation of Israel will be locked outside."

The Roman officer returned home to find his servant completely cured.

Matthew chapter 8; Mark chapter 1; Luke chapter 7; John chapter 4

Jesus Befriends Outcasts

One day Jesus was walking down a street with many of his disciples. He peered through a window and saw a man called Matthew busy working at a desk in the tax office. Jesus thought how lonely he looked. He realized that Matthew must have very few friends, if any at all. He was working as a tax collector for the Romans who were ruling Israel, and Jewish people hated the Romans. They wanted them out of their country. Tax collectors were seen to be working for the enemy.

Jesus took pity on Matthew. "Come with me," He said, with a kind smile.

Matthew felt he simply had to do as he was told. He got up, leaving his work exactly as it was, and went off with Jesus and His followers.

After that, Matthew didn't want to lose his kind, new friend. When it grew late in the day, Matthew insisted that Jesus should be his guest for supper. He invited some of the other workers from the tax office too. His usually quiet little house was filled with the happy sound of people chatting over an enjoyable meal.

Of course, when the local Pharisees heard what was going on, they didn't like it one bit. "Jesus should be sitting down to eat with important, holy people like us," they grumbled, "not common folk – and shameful traitors too!"

But Jesus explained, "I haven't come to befriend only good people. In fact, it's sinners who need me the most."

Jesus once went to dinner at the house of a Pharisee, and He wasn't very impressed. The man, called Simon, didn't give him a warm welcome at all. It was good manners for a host to greet his guests with a kiss, and give them some perfume to refresh themselves with. It was also usual for a host to give guests some water and towels so they (or a servant) could wash the dust off their feet. Simon the Pharisee did none of these things for Jesus.

However, during the meal, a woman crept into the room who had lived a very sinful life. Other people thought she was shameful and wouldn't have anything to do with her. But now, the woman knelt before Jesus and begged for forgiveness, sobbing quietly. Her falling tears wet Jesus' feet, and she used her long hair to dry them.

Then she soothed them with some expensive perfume that she had brought.

"See," Jesus said to Simon the Pharisee, "you think of yourself as a holy man and this woman as sinful, but she has shown me every kindness that you have not. It doesn't matter at all that she has done wrong in the past, she is now truly sorry and her sins are all forgiven."

And the woman went home with joy in her heart, determined to follow Jesus and live a good life from then on.

Matthew chapter 9; Mark chapter 2; Luke chapters 5, 7

213

Jesus Calms
the Storm

Jesus had been preaching to a huge crowd
by the Sea of Galilee all day. Evening
began drawing in and He felt exhausted.
Jesus needed to escape the masses of people
and rest. "Let's sail to the other side of the
lake," He said to a few of his disciples. They
all climbed into a boat, pushed off from the

shore and raised the sail.

Soon the little boat was speeding across the waters in the setting sun. Jesus sat back, his head drooped and he nodded off, lulled to sleep by the rise and fall of the sea.

While Jesus lay dreaming, the disciples were alarmed to see black clouds overhead. The wind rose, stirring up the water. The disciples hurried to roll up the sail as the gale grew stronger. It whisked the waves up into great peaks, which sent the boat rearing up and then plunging down. Water crashed over the sides. Despite their efforts to bail out the water, the waves kept breaking in, threatening to sink the boat.

Amazingly Jesus slept through it all. But now the terrified disciples woke him.

"Master!" they shouted, struggling to make their voices heard over the wailing winds. "Master, we're all going to drown!"

Jesus opened his eyes and got to his feet. His hair and clothes whipped around him as he stretched out his hands, looked up to the skies and cried, "Be still!"

At once the wind dropped, the waves died away and the clouds faded. All was peaceful again.

But now the disciples were frightened for a new reason. What kind of man could command the wind and the waves?

Matthew chapter 8; Mark chapter 4; Luke chapter 8

Two Fish and Five Loaves

There came a time when the King of Judea had John the Baptist, Jesus' good friend, thrown into prison and put to death. When Jesus heard the news, He was preaching at the Sea of Galilee. He was upset and wanted to escape the crowds who followed Him everywhere, so He could be on His own for a little while. Jesus and His twelve disciples took a little boat out across the waters. However, the hundreds of people who had come to see and hear Jesus raced around the coast, joined by more people they met on the way. The crowd was there waiting for Jesus and His friends when they arrived on the far shore.

Jesus looked at the great mass of people – many of them sick or injured, hoping desperately for a cure. His heart went out to them. "Look at them," Jesus murmured. "They are like sheep without a shepherd."

Even though Jesus was grief-stricken and exhausted, He began preaching and healing… and was still talking to the people when dusk began to fall.

"Master, you've done enough now," the disciples said, concerned for Jesus. "It's time everyone went home. We all need something to eat."

Jesus smiled wearily. "No one needs to go anywhere," He said. "You can find us all some dinner."

The disciples looked at each other in confusion. They were surrounded by at least five thousand people. How did Jesus expect the disciples to feed them all?

"We've hardly any money between all of us to buy anything for supper," Philip pointed out.

Andrew added, "The only food we have is what this lad has brought with him," and he indicated a young boy carrying a basket.

"He's got five loaves of bread and two fish, but they'll hardly go very far!"

Jesus stretched out his hands over the loaves and fish, said a blessing and broke them into pieces. Then He told his disciples, "Now share them out among everyone."

The disciples knew that they should trust Jesus, no matter what. To their amazement, there was enough bread and fish for everybody to have a hearty supper and enough left over to fill twelve baskets.

Matthew chapter 14; Mark chapter 6; Luke chapter 9; John chapter 6

Walking
on Water

It had been a long day at the Sea of
Galilee. Jesus told his weary disciples to
head for home without Him while He sent
away the thousands of people who had
gathered. "It's going to take a little while
for me to convince everyone to leave," Jesus
said to His friends with a sigh. "You start

off without me. I want to spend some time praying on my own. I'll catch up with you."

"But how will you follow us?" The disciples protested, clambering into their little boats.

"Don't worry, I'll be fine," Jesus reassured them, waving them off.

As the men sailed away, Jesus turned back to the crowds and told them it was time to go home too. No one wanted to leave Him, but eventually they began to wander away in groups. At last, Jesus was able to leave unnoticed and went a little way up a hillside. Finally, He had some peace and quiet and could pray alone. He stayed for quite a while, deep in thought, talking to God.

Meanwhile out on the Sea of Galilee, the disciples were in trouble. The wind had grown stronger, stirring up strong currents in the water and battering the little boats. The alarmed men rolled up the sails and tried to row to shore, but despite straining at the oars with all their might, the boats were being blown off course, out into dangerous open waters.

Hours passed and as the night grew darker, the wind grew wilder and the waves grew higher. The disciples realized they were lost at sea and they were terrified.

As they sat huddled in their boats, desperately waiting for the light of dawn, they saw a white glow in the darkness. It came closer and grew bigger, turning into the shape of a man. "A ghost!" they cried, even more frightened than before.

Then a voice came floating towards them on the wind.

"Don't be afraid. It's me, Jesus."

The disciples were confused. Was it really their friend and master? Or was a demon trying to trick them?

Peter spoke up bravely.

"If it's really you, Lord," he shouted back, "tell me to walk to you across the waves."

"Yes, come then," Jesus called.

Peter stood up, cautiously moved to the edge of the rocking boat and took a deep breath. The other disciples could hardly believe their eyes as Peter stepped out.

Far from sinking into the churning waters, their friend strode from wave to wave, over the swirling sea, towards Jesus.

Peter kept his eyes fixed on Jesus, not daring to look down. But when he was within a couple of steps of Jesus, his curiosity got the better of him and he glanced down. The moment he saw the frothing foam beneath his feet, his courage deserted him and he plunged down into the dark, cold waters. "Help me, Jesus!" Peter screamed in a panic. "I'm sinking!"

Jesus reached out and grabbed Peter's hand, heaving him up. "Don't doubt me," He said. "Have more faith." Jesus guided his friend back to the boats and suddenly the wind died down and the waves calmed.

The disciples had watched everything in amazement. "You really are the Son of God," they said, falling in awe at Jesus' feet.

Matthew chapter 14; Mark chapter 6; John chapter 6

A Visit to
Martha and Mary

Jesus once stopped in a little village called Bethany. A woman called Martha who lived in the village invited Jesus and His disciples into her house to rest and eat. They were grateful and accepted her kind offer.

Martha introduced the men to her sister, Mary. Then she showed Jesus and His

friends to where they could sit, and began
bustling about. First she disappeared into
the kitchen and brought out bowls of water
and towels so that they could freshen up
from the dust of the road. Then she went to
fetch pitchers of juice and drinking cups to
quench their thirst. Back to the kitchen she
dashed to prepare trays of hot drinks and
plates of food.

Meanwhile, Mary
had made herself
comfortable at
Jesus' feet. While
Martha was racing
about, seeing to
their guests, Mary
sat and gazed up at

the great preacher, listening intently to every word He said.

"Mary, it would be nice if you gave me a hand," Martha whispered, carrying another tray of food.

But her sister didn't follow her back to the kitchen. Instead, Martha found herself cooking dinner for thirteen guests all on her own. How fed up she felt! After all, she would like to be sitting and chatting with the famous preacher and His twelve friends. But somebody had to prepare the food, and her sister wasn't going to do it.

So Martha continued to make trips back and forth from the kitchen, carrying in starters, main courses and desserts, and clearing away tray after tray of empty plates, bowls and cups.

By the time everyone had finished eating and Martha had cleared everything away, Jesus, the disciples and Mary were deep in conversation. Martha had missed the start of the discussion so she couldn't really understand what they were talking about. And her guests had all spread out so much in the room that there was hardly space for her to sit down.

How left out Martha felt! As she looked at her sister sitting right next to Jesus, having done nothing at all, she felt a lump rise in her throat and tears begin to prick her eyes.

"Lord," she suddenly burst out in frustration, "how could you let my sister just sit there lazily and do nothing? Why didn't you tell her to get up and help?"

"My poor Martha, thank you so much for your kindness," Jesus said, getting up to comfort the upset woman. "But you have prepared so many different dishes for us when just one would have been enough. Your sister has chosen to pay attention to me in the best way of all – listening. I can't possibly tell her off for that."

Luke chapter 10

Lazarus
is Awoken

A messenger brought urgent news to Jesus from Martha and Mary, the two women he had stayed with in the village of Bethany. Their brother, Lazarus, had fallen seriously ill and they feared he was dying.

Jesus had made firm friends with the two sisters and their brother, and was fond of them. But to the disciples' surprise He didn't rush off when He received the message. "Lazarus will be fine," Jesus told them. "God has made him ill on purpose in order to show His glorious power through me."

Jesus stayed where He was, preaching and healing for another two days. On the third day He told the disciples that He was at last heading back to Bethany. "I have to wake Lazarus," He explained.

"But master," protested the disciples, rather puzzled, "if Lazarus is sleeping, won't he wake up on his own?"

"Lazarus is dead," Jesus announced calmly. "And I am glad I wasn't there to save him because now I can work a miracle that will give you more faith in me."

By the time Jesus arrived at Bethany Lazarus had been dead for four days. As he approached the sisters' house, a red-eyed Martha came out. "Oh Lord," she sobbed, "if only you had been here, Lazarus would not have died." Wiping her tears, she looked at Jesus. "But I know that God will grant you anything you ask for," she whispered.

Jesus was moved by Martha's faith. Holding her gaze, He asked, "Do you accept that anyone who believes in me and dies will live again? That anyone who believes in me and lives will never die?"

"I do, my Lord," replied Martha.

"Then fetch your sister and show me where you have buried your brother," Jesus said gently.

Martha hurried to fetch Mary, and together they and their grief-stricken friends accompanied Jesus to Lazarus' tomb. He had been laid to rest in a cave with a large stone set across the entrance.

"Roll away the rock," Jesus ordered.

The sisters were shocked. "But master, he has been dead for four days," said Martha. "His body will smell."

Jesus waved away their protests. As everyone helped clear the entrance, He started to pray. "Father, you always hear me and answer me," Jesus said, "and I thank you with all my heart. Now I am asking for something that will help everyone believe that it's you who have sent me."

Jesus shut his eyes and stood very still.

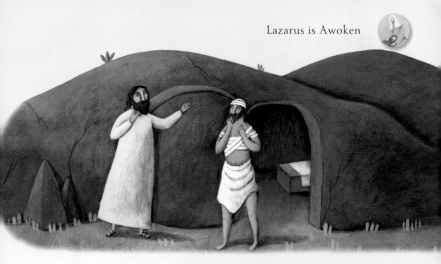

Then his firm, clear voice echoed into the cave. "Lazarus, come out!" He commanded.

After a while, everyone heard a shuffling sound and a shrouded figure came staggering out of the cave.

"Don't be afraid, unwrap your brother," Jesus urged Mary and Martha.

Hardly daring to breathe, they did so. Lazarus was alive and well again.

John chapters 11 to 27

Jesus Teaches through Stories

Jesus often preached about God and the way to happiness in Heaven by telling people stories with hidden meanings, called parables. He once told a parable about a farmer who was sowing seed in his field. As he went, he scattered seed all around him so it would grow.

"Some of the seed fell onto the footpath," said Jesus, "so it didn't sink into the soil and birds swooped down and ate it up. These seeds never had a chance to grow."

Jesus went on, "Other seeds fell onto rocky, stony ground. They started to grow, but couldn't put down deep, strong roots. Under the hot summer sun, the young crops couldn't take up enough moisture from the earth and they withered, scorched and died."

Jesus continued, "Some seeds landed on patches of thorny weeds. The crops grew but the weeds grew up faster and choked

them. However, some
seeds fell onto good,
rich soil and they
grew into tall,
plentiful crops."

Jesus didn't tell His listeners
what the parable meant. He
wanted them to try to understand
it for themselves. That way, they would
really think about what Jesus had told them
and they wouldn't forget His message.

Later Jesus explained to His disciples.
"The seed is the Word of God. The footpath
stands for people who hear the Word of
God but who don't take it in. The devil will
swoop down and seize it from them so they
forget. The seed that falls on rocky ground

stands for people who listen to the Word of God but don't take it in. When they are faced with problems, their difficulties overcome them. The seed that falls among weeds stands for people who hear the Word of God but get distracted by selfish habits and desires. Finally, the seed that falls onto good soil stands for people who take the Word of God into their hearts. Over time it grows there and bears fruit."

Jesus warned everyone to listen hard to His parables. "No one buys a lamp and hides its light," he said. "So don't ignore my teachings. Everything I am telling you will one day prove to be true."

Matthew chapter 13; Mark chapter 4; Luke chapter 8

The Good Samaritan

Jesus always surprised people by knowing Jewish religious rules inside out and back to front. Many religious leaders and holy men who had spent their whole lives studying the laws were jealous of Jesus' knowledge. So they would ask tricky questions to try to catch Him out.

One day a lawyer came to Jesus and asked, "What must I do to win eternal life?"

"What does the law tell you to do?" Jesus answered simply.

"To love God with all my heart and soul, and to love my neighbour as I love myself," the lawyer reeled off smugly, showing off his knowledge.

"Exactly," said Jesus. "If you already know, why are you asking me?"

"Ah, but who is my neighbour?" the man asked, feeling confident that he had posed a question far too difficult for Jesus to answer.

"Let me tell you a story," Jesus said, without a moment's hesitation. "There was once a man travelling on the road from Jerusalem to Jericho. Suddenly a group of bandits sprang out from behind some rocks and attacked him. There was no one around to hear the traveller's cries for help. The bandits beat him, robbed him of all his possessions and left him for dead.

"After a while, a priest came walking down the road," Jesus continued. "He wondered what a bundle of rags was doing in the middle of the road and went over to have a look. As soon as the priest saw that the heap was actually a man lying bleeding in the dust, he quickly crossed to the other side of

the road. He didn't want to
know what had happened
or have anything to do
with it."

The lawyer gasped,
"How could such a
holy man not help
someone in need?"

"The next traveller to
approach was a Levite," Jesus carried on.
"This man is sure to help," said the
Lawyer. Jews from the tribe of Levi were so
god-fearing that priests were always chosen
from among them.

"The Levite shuddered in disgust when
he saw the battered and bruised man barely
alive," Jesus continued. "Like the priest

before him, he crossed to the far side of the road and walked away."

Now the lawyer was really shocked. A holy Levite should have known better.

"Next, a Samaritan passed by," Jesus announced.

The lawyer pulled a face. Samaritans were the people who had been sent to live in Israel when the Jews were taken away as slaves by the Babylonians. The Jews hated the Samaritans for taking their land. They also looked down on the Samaritans because they weren't God's Chosen People and often didn't worship God at all. The lawyer thought the Samaritan probably went over to see if there was anything left to steal!

But Jesus continued, "The Samaritan was appalled when he saw the injured man and rushed to help. He gave the poor man some water, heaved him up onto his donkey and hurried to the nearest town. There he paid an innkeeper to take him in and look after him until he was better."

The lawyer was flabbergasted.

"Now which of the three travellers would you say was the neighbour of the attacked man?" Jesus asked.

"The one who helped him," stuttered the lawyer.

"Right," said Jesus. "Now go and behave like the Samaritan."

Luke chapter 10

A Story of Forgiveness

Jesus told a story about a farmer who had two sons. The farmer was teaching his sons all about farming so that when he died, they could take over. However one day, the younger son approached his father with an idea.

"I've been thinking, father," he said

nervously. "I'm grown up and it's time I saw a bit of the world. It would help if I could have my share of the farm now in cash."

The farmer loved his sons dearly and he didn't even have to think about the decision. He counted hundreds of silver coins into bags and handed them to the excited lad.

"Thank you, father," he said, packing his bags to set off. "You won't regret it."

And the farmer watched with tears in his eyes as his younger son left home.

For a while the farmer's son had a wonderful time. He lived like a prince, visiting the finest cities, eating out every night and going to parties. He was surrounded by people who wanted to be his friend, but the problem was they helped him spend all his money. When the silver was gone, his friends vanished too. The young man found himself alone and far from home, without even a few pennies to buy a loaf of bread. To make matters worse, a dreadful drought swept through the land, causing a terrible famine. The farmer's son couldn't even beg for food because no one had enough for themselves. Luckily, he found a job as a pig-keeper. But the wages were pitiful. He had hardly enough money left to buy food after paying his rent. Some days he was so hungry he nearly ate the food for the pigs!

One day, he decided enough was enough. "I want to go home," he groaned. "I'll beg my father for his forgiveness for being such an idiot. He's bound to be furious, but maybe if I grovel, he'll let me stay and work as one of his farm labourers."

The miserable, ragged young man arrived home and couldn't believe how overjoyed his father was to see him. "I've worried about you and missed you every day, son," the farmer cried, hugging and kissing him.

The ashamed son sobbed as he told his father what had happened.

"Never mind," the farmer said, to his

251

son's utter astonishment. "You're back home now and we're together again. That's all that matters."

Later, the farmer's elder son came home from a hard day's work in the fields to find a party in full swing. The neighbours had been invited over to celebrate, and a feast had been prepared. There was music, dancing and the people were drinking wine.

"Whatever's going on here?" he gasped, and one of the servants explained what had happened.

The farmer swung his elder son round in a jig. "Rejoice!" he cried. "Your little brother has finally come back home!"

"What do you mean, 'rejoice'?" the elder son spat, completely furious. "I've stayed with you all these years, working my fingers to the bone, and you've never given me so much as a thank you – let alone thrown me a party! Then HE turns up, having wasted most of your fortune, and you're celebrating how wonderful he is!"

"You have no idea how much your faithfulness means to me," the farmer said to his elder son, drawing him close in a hug. "Everything I have, I give to you. But today is a day to be glad, for your brother was lost and gone forever, but he has come home."

Luke chapter 15

Jesus and
the Children

The twelve disciples were travelling with
Jesus along a road one day. They
began to fall behind, squabbling among
themselves. Their argument was about
which of them would be the greatest in the
Kingdom of Heaven. They thought that
Jesus couldn't hear them, but He did. They

were saying things like, "Well, I should be the greatest because I'm Jesus' oldest friend…" And, "I should be the greatest because I've performed the most miracles…" And, "No, I'm sure I'll be the greatest because I pray the most often."

Jesus didn't stop them, He just listened to every word. But later on when they had reached their destination and sat down to rest, He asked, "So what were you all talking about on the road then?"

The disciples felt embarrassed to think that Jesus had heard them trying to outdo each other. No one admitted a thing, but Jesus knew all about what had gone on. "If you really want to be the greatest in God's eyes, you must put others before yourself,"

He told the red-faced men. Jesus reached out to a little girl who was passing by and drew her towards Him. "You must be like this child," He said. "You must have simple, honest values and take genuine delight in helping others. Never look down on children, for they are selfless and giving. They are among the greatest in Heaven."

However, it didn't take long for the disciples to forget what Jesus had told them. A few weeks later, Jesus had been preaching all day long when a group of people with young children approached, asking Him to bless them. Some of the children clung to their parents, while others were playful and pestered Jesus for attention. Jesus' disciples were sure that this would be annoying for

the weary preacher and they began to shoo
the children away. But Jesus stopped his
friends. "Let the children come to me," He
instructed. "After all, the Kingdom of
Heaven belongs to them." Jesus picked up
the smallest child and let others scramble
onto his lap, blessing them all. "Unless you
are pure and wholehearted like these
children," He warned his disciples
once more, "you will never
see God."

Matthew chapters 18, 19; Mark chapters 9, 10;
Luke chapters 9, 18

Jesus the Good Shepherd

Jesus once said to a crowd that had gathered to hear him speak, "What would a shepherd do if wolves attacked the sheep in his flock? If he was a hired shepherd, doing his job only for the money, he wouldn't stay and fight off the wolves. He would run away and save himself, leaving the sheep to be eaten. I am not like that shepherd, I am the good shepherd. I will look after my sheep even if it means I have to die for them. I have flocks in other places too, which I need to gather so I can look after all my animals together. My sheep know my voice, they will listen to me and follow me anywhere. It's because I will give up my life for my sheep willingly – for love, not any other reward – that God loves me and will give me my life back again."

Many of Jesus' listeners were puzzled by these words. "He must be mad," some of them mumbled. "Do you think it's demons inside Him that are talking?"

But others knew that Jesus was trying to get them to understand something important. "Of course He's not mad!" they insisted, even though they weren't sure what Jesus meant. "How could someone possessed by demons miraculously heal people?"

What Jesus wanted everyone to know was that He genuinely cared for them. Not just for Jewish people, but for people everywhere who wanted to follow God. He was also warning that He was ready to die for everybody, if that is what He had to do. Jesus was explaining that it is only by loving everyone and willingly helping other people in this world, that God will reward us with new life in the next.

John chapter 10

Jesus Warns
of the Future

There came a rare moment when Jesus found Himself alone with His disciples, walking along a road. He took the opportunity to talk with them. "I sometimes call myself 'the Son of Man'," He began. "What do you think I mean by that?"

"Some people believe you are John the

Baptist," one disciple shrugged.

"Or the prophet Elijah come back from the dead," another suggested.

"Or a new, greater prophet," a third said.

"But who do you think I am?" He asked.

"I think you are the Messiah, the Son of the Living God," Peter announced firmly.

"Then God has blessed you," Jesus said to Peter. "Your name means 'rock', and you are the rock on which

I will build my church. I will give you the keys to Heaven, and whatever rules you set on Earth will also stand in Heaven."

Jesus turned to everyone and said gravely, "I must warn you all that things are soon going to get very difficult. The time is drawing near when I must go to Jerusalem. I will go through much suffering," Jesus gave a sigh. "And eventually I will be put to death." The disciples gasped, but Jesus held up his hands to silence them. "However, three days later, I will come back to life."

The disciples were amazed.

"Are you ready to follow me into hardship and sorrow – even to die for me?" Jesus asked his friends. "If you are, I cannot grant you a reward in this world, but I can promise you joy in the next."

Jesus' friends walked on with heavy, but determined, hearts.

Matthew chapter 16; Mark chapter 8; Luke chapter 9

The First Palm Sunday

It was the week before the great feast of Passover. Jews from far-off lands travelled to Jerusalem for the celebrations, which lasted several days. Jewish holy men such as the chief priests and Pharisees were waiting to see if Jesus would dare visit the city too. They had been plotting for a long time to arrest and execute the preacher who they thought was stirring up the people and leading them astray. The Jewish leaders thought Jesus might enter Jerusalem unnoticed by mingling among the crowds, so they sent spies through Jerusalem to see if they could spot Him.

However Jesus was planning to arrive quite openly. When He and His disciples were a little way off, on the Mount of Olives, Jesus sent two of His friends into the village of Bethphage to find a donkey for him to ride. "You will find one tethered to a doorway," He told them. "Untie it and bring it to me. If anyone objects, just explain that it's me who needs it and they won't stop you."

The disciples found the donkey, just as He had said. When the owners heard who wanted it, they brought it to Jesus themselves. They even threw their cloaks onto its back to make a comfortable saddle for Him to sit on. The little animal had never been ridden before, but it stood calm and willing as Jesus climbed onto it.

Jesus patted the donkey's head, then set off for the city of Jerusalem. When people along the way saw Him coming, they cheered, sang and danced for joy. The ancient prophets had said that the Messiah would ride into Jerusalem on a donkey. And so the people realized that Jesus was claiming openly for the first time that He was the saviour they had been waiting for.

"Hosanna!" they shouted, lining the donkey's path with their cloaks and palm leaves. "Blessed is He who comes in the name of the Lord! Hosanna in the highest!"

People jammed the streets to welcome Jesus all the way into Jerusalem.

"This is outrageous!" the furious Pharisees bellowed at Jesus. "You're making these people think you're the Messiah!"

"Even if they were quiet," Jesus replied, "the stones themselves would cry out to greet me."

Matthew chapter 21; Mark chapter 11; Luke chapter 19; John chapters 11, 12

Jesus and the Temple Traders

As all good Jews did at the feast of Passover, Jesus went to pray at the great temple. He expected to see the courtyards filled with respectful worshippers deep in prayer, moving quietly about so as not to disturb others. Instead, Jesus was horrified to find the sacred building being used as a market-place.

Everywhere He looked, there were
stallholders selling doves and other animals
for sacrifices. They cried out their wares,
competing for business. People bartered
with them, trying to get the best prices,
while doves cooed and lambs bleated.
Among the stalls were money-changers,
haggling with worshippers and counting
out foreign money into Jewish shekels. All
the traders were charging unfair prices,
and the worshippers had no choice but to
pay. Everyone had to offer a sacrifice and
give shekels to the temple funds at Passover.
Meanwhile, city traders were using the
temple courtyards and corridors to get from
one side of Jerusalem to another.

As Jesus stood amid the hubbub, he grew furious. Suddenly, He began sending the traders' tables flying into the air, kicking down stalls, smashing dove cages open and ripping animal tethers loose. "This is the house of God, but you have turned it into a robbers' den!" He yelled, clearing the temple of everyone except for genuine worshippers.

It wasn't long before the courtyards were full again. This time, with people who had come to hear Jesus preach.

Matthew chapter 21;
Luke chapter 19

Jesus Against the Authorities

Every day of Passover week Jesus stood in the temple preaching to huge crowds and healing many people too. The Jewish leaders were enraged. "Who gives you the right to say and do these things?" they demanded. "Listen to what the people are saying about you – they think you are the

Messiah! We are warning you to stop."
They sent holy men such as the Pharisees
and Sadducees to try to make Jesus break
the law in some way so they could arrest
Him. But Jesus waged a war of words on
them and won every time.

"Holy men such as the Pharisees say
that you should follow the rules of Moses,"
He told everyone one day. "This is right,
so listen to what they say. But don't do as
they do because they don't practise what
they preach!"

People in the crowd began to argue
angrily with each other – the Jewish
leaders and their followers on one side, and
Jesus and His disciples on the other.

Jesus continued, "Everything the holy

men do is for show. They say aloud long prayers in public so everyone can admire them. They wear fancy robes so they stand out in the crowd. They sit at the front at the synagogue and expect to be addressed as 'Teacher'. But I say you have only one teacher – your Father in Heaven, and under Him, everyone is equal. Anyone who thinks they are better than others will one day find themselves the lowest. And anyone who serves others will one day find themselves the greatest."

Jesus criticized the Jewish elders in many other ways, leaving the people in uproar as they debated whether He was right or wrong. "Look at that lady over there," Jesus tried to explain. He pointed to a tiny, bent-over old woman in tatty clothes, shuffling to the temple collection box. With gnarled, trembling fingers, she dropped in a couple of copper coins and prayed. "That old woman is better than all the Jewish leaders," Jesus announced. "They only give what they can afford to charity, leaving plenty for themselves. This woman has hardly anything, but she has still given to God."

The Jewish leaders were determined to somehow seize Jesus. Every day He was surrounded by people in the temple. And every night He stayed outside the city, at Bethany. Jesus was safe for now.

Matthew chapters 21, 23; Mark chapter 12; Luke chapters 19, 21

The Last Supper

The Jewish leaders were extremely frustrated at their failure to get rid of Jesus. One night they gathered at the house of the chief priest, Caiaphas, for an emergency meeting. They were in the middle of discussing what they could do next when there was a knock at the door.

A servant ushered in a most unexpected guest. It was Judas Iscariot, one of Jesus' twelve disciples and closest friends.

"I'm here because I can give you what you want," he said, his eyes glinting coldly. "Jesus of Nazareth – how much is He worth to you?"

The Jewish officials didn't know what had made Judas become a traitor – and they didn't care either. They could hardly believe their good luck. They put their heads together for a few moments and then announced, "Thirty pieces of silver."

Without a word, Judas held out his hand and Caiaphas counted out the coins. From then on, Judas stayed by Jesus' side, waiting for the opportunity to betray Him.

Mysteriously, Jesus knew everything.
With a heavy heart, He prepared for one
last meal with his disciples – the Passover
supper. He organized a room in secret, so
that the Jewish leaders would not find out
where He was, and only told His twelve
friends about it at the last minute.

The disciples were in a very serious
mood as they gathered together. After all,
Jesus had warned them two days earlier
that He was about to fall into the hands of
His enemies and be put to death. As
everything Jesus said came true, they were
extremely worried.

While they settled at the table, Jesus
wrapped a towel around his waist and filled
a bowl with water. The disciples were

shocked to realize He was going to wash the dust from their feet – a job usually done by the very lowliest servant. Peter was especially shocked and tried to stop Jesus kneeling before him, but Jesus insisted. "I am setting you all an example," Jesus said afterwards. "Always put others before yourself."

Then it was time for dinner. Jesus took a loaf of bread and asked for God's blessing over it. "This is my body," He said with great sadness, "which will be given up for you." He broke the bread and gave it to all the disciples to eat. Then Jesus poured a cup of wine and asked for God's blessing over that too. "This is my blood," He announced gravely, "the sign of a new promise from

God. My blood will be spilt so that
everyone's sins will be forgiven." One by
one, the disciples took the cup and drank.

Then Jesus gestured for everyone to
begin sharing out the different dishes on the
table. As they did so, He gave a deep sigh.

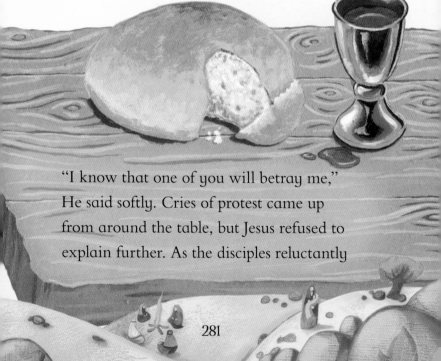

"I know that one of you will betray me,"
He said softly. Cries of protest came up
from around the table, but Jesus refused to
explain further. As the disciples reluctantly

turned back to eating, Peter murmured to John, who was sitting closest to Jesus, "Ask Him which of us He means."

John leaned over and spoke in Jesus' ear.

He whispered back, "The one to whom I will give this piece of bread."

John told Peter, and they watched as Jesus tore some bread and offered it to Judas Iscariot. "Do whatever you have to," Jesus told His disloyal friend, "but do it quickly."

And without a word Judas got up from the table and left the room.

Matthew chapter 26; Mark chapter 14; Luke chapter 22; John chapter 13

The Garden
of Gethsemane

After Jesus had shared His last supper
with the disciples, He sat back and
looked around at His dear friends. "I give
you a new commandment," He said. "Love
each other as I have loved you. By doing
this, everyone will know that you are my
followers."

"Lord, you've been talking all night as if you're leaving us," Peter protested.

"Yes," Jesus said gently. "I am going away, and where I am going you won't be able to follow me – for a while, at least."

"Why can't I follow you now?" Peter cried out. "I am ready to die for you!"

But Jesus smiled sadly. "Are you really, my friend?" He asked. "By the time this night is out and the cock has crowed three times at dawn, you will have denied three times that you even know me."

"Never," Peter said, choking with sorrow. "Never." And all the disciples agreed strongly.

"Don't be upset," Jesus tried to comfort them. "I am going to prepare a place for

you in my Father's house. And I will return
to you for a short while, before I have to go
away again for good. Even then when you
will no longer be able to see me, I will
always live in your hearts. Later, when the
time is right, you will follow and we will be
together again. Until then, do what I have
done tonight as a way of remembering me.
Be at peace, and be happy for me that I am
going to be with my Father."

Jesus looked around at His friends'
gloomy faces.

"Now come," He said gently. "Let's go
to the Mount of Olives. I would like to pray
in the Garden of Gethsemane for a while."

As they walked through the moonlight
together, Jesus gave the disciples many more

important instructions. He knew He only had a short time left in which to talk to them. When they finally reached the entrance to the Garden of Gethsemane, Jesus saw that the anxious men were exhausted. "Rest here while I go and pray," He told most of them. But He turned to Peter, James and John and said, "I know you are tired, but would you come with me?"

The three were only too pleased to keep Jesus company. They had never seen Him look so strained and troubled before.

"My heart feels like it's breaking," Jesus sighed heavily when they had gone a little way. "Will you stay while I pray?"

Peter, James and John watched as Jesus sank to his knees, His head in His hands.

"Father!" He cried
silently. Jesus prayed
that perhaps He might
not have to face the suffering
He knew lay ahead.

After a long while, Jesus
turned to Peter, James and John
but saw they had fallen asleep.

So Jesus prayed again. He felt the sins of
all the world weighing on His shoulders and
He knew the full horror of what was to
come.

Once more Jesus turned to his friends,
but they were still asleep.

And Jesus prayed again, willingly
accepting the suffering He had to face, so

that all people could one day reach God.

At last Jesus finished praying. Peter, James and John were still asleep. But at that moment Judas Iscariot arrived, accompanied by a band of guards. At the noise of guards' swords and chains and the light from their flaming torches, the disciples woke up, startled. "Master," Judas said calmly, greeting Jesus with his usual kiss.

At that pre-arranged sign, the guards grabbed Jesus. After a brief commotion and panic, the disciples fled for their lives into the darkness.

Matthew chapter 26; Mark chapter 14; Luke chapter 22; John chapters 13, 14, 18

Jesus
on Trial

Inside Caiaphas' mansion, Jesus was quizzed by Annas, the former high priest. What did He think about ancient holy writings? What miracles did He claim to have worked? Who did He think He was?

Jesus refused to answer and was marched to a room full of Jewish officials. They had witnesses who they had paid to lie, accusing Jesus of saying and doing things that were against Jewish law. But the witnesses couldn't get their stories straight!

Finally Caiaphas hissed, "I order you to tell us, under solemn oath, whether you think you are the Son of God."

"I am," He said with grace, "and one day you will see the Son of Man seated at the right hand of the Father in Heaven."

"Blasphemy!" roared Caiaphas, a satisfied gleam in his eyes. Blasphemy was the crime of lying against God for which the punishment was death.

In triumph, the Jewish elders had Jesus blindfolded. They slapped and kicked Him, shouting, "Prophesy for us now, Messiah.

Guess who hit you!" And in the morning, they had Jesus brought in front of the Roman governor, Pontius Pilate. Only he could approve an execution.

The news spread around the city and an enormous crowd gathered outside.

Pilate asked Jesus many more questions. Are you really a king? Have you been plotting against the Roman government? Have you been planning a rebellion?

Perplexed, Pilate couldn't find that Jesus had done anything wrong. He ordered that Jesus also be questioned by Herod, the ruler of Galilee, who was in Jerusalem at that time. But Herod couldn't find Jesus guilty of anything either. Even Pilate's wife told him that she had had a dream in which Jesus of

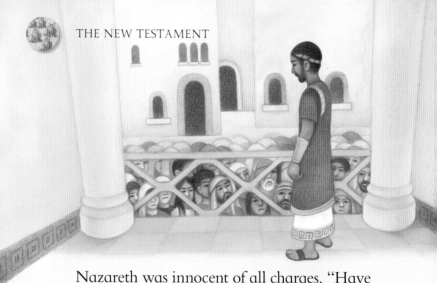

Nazareth was innocent of all charges. "Have nothing further to do with him," she advised her husband.

Pilate made his decision. He went out onto the balcony of his judgement hall and announced to the waiting crowds, "This man has done nothing to deserve death. He shall be whipped and let go." And Jesus was dragged off for His punishment.

Meanwhile the Jewish officials had

mingled with the crowds, persuading them that Jesus was guilty of blasphemy. As Pilate turned to go back into his Judgement Hall, people sent up cries of, "Kill him! Kill Jesus of Nazareth!"

The Roman governor was deeply disturbed, but he did not know what for. Suddenly he had an idea. Pilate remembered that it was Passover and there was a custom for the governor to release one prisoner of the people's choice. In the cells was a murderer called Barabbas. Pilate felt sure that the people would rather have Jesus released than a violent killer.

"Who shall I pardon – Barabbas or Jesus of Nazareth?" Pilate asked the crowd.

He couldn't believe his ears when the

shouts came back, "Barabbas!"

Pilate ordered that Jesus be brought in front of him once more. He had been whipped until blood poured down His back. The guards had mocked him as the King of the Jews, too, by pressing a crown of thorns onto His head and throwing a cloak around his shoulders.

Now the crowd jeered too.

Pilate had had enough. He called for water and a towel, and washed his hands in front of everyone. "I cleanse myself of this man's blood," he announced.

Then Barabbas was released and Jesus was led away to be crucified.

Matthew chapters 26, 27; Mark chapters 14, 15;
Luke chapters 22, 23; John chapters 18, 19

The Crucifixion

Jesus had withstood being marched about in chains, hours of angry questioning, a beating from the Jewish officials, and being brutally whipped by Pilate's guards. The crown of thorns was still pressed into His head, sending blood trickling down His pain-filled face.

Two Roman soldiers lifted a huge, solid wooden cross over Jesus' shoulder – so heavy that He nearly collapsed from the weight of it. Then Jesus staggered onwards, through the streets of Jerusalem and towards the hill outside the city where He and two other criminals were to be executed.

Thousands of people lined the way, watching the procession. Jesus willed Himself forwards, heavy step after heavy step. But eventually He crashed into the dust, utterly exhausted. The angry guards dragged a strong man from the crowd called Simon of Cyrene and ordered him to carry the cross instead.

People in the crowd yelled insults and spat on Jesus as He stumbled by. But Jesus caught sight of the sorrowful faces of many friends He had made too. Many of the women were weeping. "Don't cry for me," Jesus said, "but for yourselves, your children and for the destruction that is to come."

Eventually they reached the place for the execution. It was called Golgotha, meaning 'place of the skull'. A soldier made Jesus lie down on the cross, and long nails were hammered into His hands and feet. "Father forgive them, for they don't know what they are doing," Jesus moaned. A notice was fixed above his head which said 'Jesus of Nazareth, King of the Jews' in three languages. "It shouldn't say that," some

Jewish officials objected. "It should say 'This man said he was the King of the Jews'."

But the Roman governor, Pilate, boomed, "I ordered it to be written just like that and that is the way it will stay!"

The Jewish officials mocked as Jesus' cross was hoisted up high. "You said you're the Son of God – so save yourself!"

As the two criminals were raised on crosses either side of Jesus, one sneered, "Yes, save yourself and save us too!"

"How dare you!" the second thief groaned. "We deserve this, but Jesus is innocent. Lord, remember me when you reach your kingdom."

"I promise you," whispered Jesus, "today you will be with me in paradise."

Even though it was midday, darkness suddenly fell over the land. Close by at the foot of the cross, was Jesus' heartbroken mother, and His close friends including John, Mary Magdalene and Salome.

"Mother, take care of John as if he were your own son," Jesus murmered. "John, look after my mother as if she were your own."

Jesus hung in agony on the cross for three long hours. Then He lifted His head and cried aloud, "My God! Why have you abandoned me?" Somebody rushed to lift a stick with a sponge on the end that had been dipped in wine so He could have a drink. Jesus cried out again, "Father, I give up my spirit into your hands. It is finished." And His head drooped.

At that very moment, the earth rumbled and shook, and rocks split open. People said that the great curtain in the temple ripped from top to bottom. Others said they saw graves open and spirits rise from them.

A Roman officer at the foot of the cross looked up and gasped, "This man truly was the Son of God."

Matthew chapter 27; Mark chapter 15; Luke chapter 23; John chapter 19

The First Easter

The evening after Jesus had been put to death, a wealthy Jew called Joseph of Arimathea begged Pontius Pilate to allow him to bury Jesus' body. Pilate agreed. So Joseph went with his friend, Nicodemus, back to Golgotha, where women were still weeping at the foot of His cross. Gently,

Joseph and Nicodemus lifted Jesus' poor, bleeding body down. They wrapped Him in a linen shroud with burial spices and, accompanied by the sobbing women, took Him to a nearby cemetery. There the two men laid Jesus in a small, cave-like tomb that Joseph had already paid for, and rolled a heavy stone across the entrance. Full of grief and with nothing else to do, they left.

Meanwhile, some Jewish officials had been to see Pilate. "Jesus of Nazareth said He would rise up again after three days," they told the Roman governor. "Have soldiers guard His tomb so no one can steal the body, then tell everyone that He's miraculously come back to life." Pilate nodded and sent the men away.

Pilate's guards sat outside Jesus' tomb through the night of that first Good Friday – nothing happened. They kept watch all the next day and again nobody came. But as dawn broke on the Sabbath, the third day, the earth suddenly shook so violently that it knocked the soldiers off their feet. A white light blazed out of the sky and shone over the tomb. Through the glare, the terrified soldiers watched the glowing figure of a man roll away the massive stone from the tomb entrance. The soldiers were scared by what they saw and fled for their lives.

Not long afterwards a group of grieving women arrived at the cemetery to pay their respects at the tomb. They included Jesus' friends Mary Magdalene, Mary the mother

of James and John, Salome and Joanna.
When they saw that the soldiers were gone
and the stone had been rolled away, they
screamed in horror. Someone
must have stolen
Jesus' body!

Inside the tomb
where Jesus' body
should have been,
two shining figures
were sitting. "Why
are you looking
for the living
among the dead?"
the figures said. "Don't you remember that
the Son of Man said He would rise on the
third day?"

Mary Magdalene raced to fetch the disciples Peter and John. When the two men saw the empty tomb they were full of anger. They went off to try to find out who had taken the body. Mary sank down outside the tomb, sobbing. Then suddenly she sensed someone behind her. Mary spun round and, through her tears she saw a blurry figure whom she thought must be the cemetery gardener. "Why are you weeping?" the man asked.

"If you moved the body," she begged, "please tell me where to."

The man said just one word.

"Mary."

Mary's heart stood still. Suddenly, she recognized the man – it was Jesus!

"Go now," Jesus said softly, as Mary fell at His feet, gazing up at Him in wonder. "Find the disciples and tell them that I will soon be returning to my Father."

Meanwhile, the other women who had seen the empty tomb were hurrying homewards when all at once, a man appeared out of nowhere on the road in front of them. "Good morning," He said.

The women were amazed and couldn't believe who they were hearing and seeing.

"Don't be afraid," Jesus said. "Go and tell my disciples to travel to Galilee and I will meet them there soon."

Matthew chapters 27, 28; Mark chapter 16; Luke chapters 23, 24; John chapters 19, 20

Jesus and
Doubting Thomas

Late morning on the third day after Jesus'
death, Mary Magdalene burst into the
room where the grieving disciples sat
together. "I have seen Jesus!" she cried,
flushed with excitement, and told them
everything that had happened at the tomb.
But as much as the disciples wanted to

believe her, they couldn't.

Meanwhile, two of Jesus' disciples were on their way from Jerusalem to the nearby village of Emmaus. As they walked with heavy hearts, a stranger joined them and began talking. To the disciples' astonishment, the stranger didn't seem to have heard anything of the events everyone was talking about – the death of Jesus and the disappearance of His body. However, he seemed to know the ancient holy writings very well and began explaining them.

"Don't you know that the holy men of old said that the Messiah would have to suffer to win glory?"

Later on the disciples shared a meal with the stranger and he blessed some bread,

broke it into pieces and gave it to them.
It was only then that they realized who he
really was. "Jesus!" they gasped in
astonishment. And at that moment, He
disappeared.

The disciples hurried back to the city
and went straight to tell the others – only to
find that Jesus had appeared to Peter too!

Everyone began talking at once, full of
excitement and asking to hear the stories
again and again. No one noticed the
newcomer arrive in their midst.

"Peace be with you," said Jesus, as
everyone stood back in fear as though He
was a ghost. "Don't be frightened," He
said, "it's me. Look – here are the wounds
on my hands and feet."

But one disciple was missing – Thomas. When his friends told him what had happened he didn't believe it. Eight days later everyone was gathered again to talk and pray. Halfway through the meeting, Jesus appeared once more. "See for yourself, Thomas," He said. "Come and touch my wounds. Have faith – it's true."

Thomas broke down. "My Lord, it's really you," he sobbed.

"Bless you for believing," Jesus said gently. "But even more blessed are those who won't see me and yet will still believe."

Matthew chapter 28; Mark chapter 16;
Luke chapter 24; John chapter 20

The Stranger
on the Beach

One evening, some of the disciples gathered at the Sea of Galilee. Peter wanted to take a little boat out and go fishing, just as he used to do in the days when he was a fisherman. Soon he and his friends, including James, John, Thomas and Nathaniel, were sailing out into open waters under a starry sky. How free and peaceful it felt – a welcome relief from the terrible events in the city in recent weeks.

All night, the disciples waited for fish to fill their nets, but when dawn came, they were all empty.

Then a voice floated across the waves. "Have you caught anything?"

Peering into the distance, the disciples could see the figure of a man on the shore.

"No, nothing." they yelled back.

"Try dropping your nets to the right side of the boat," came the voice.

The disciples thought it was worth a try. They soon felt their nets become heavy and they could hardly lift them.

Peter, James and John looked at each

other and they remembered a time in the past when exactly the same thing had happened. "It's Jesus!" they exclaimed.

Peter couldn't wait to finish hauling in the catch and sail to shore, so he dived straight into the water and swam to be the first to reach Jesus.

Before long, Peter and the rest of the friends joined Jesus on the shore, and gathered around a little fire on the beach.

They sat roasting fish for breakfast, and it was just like old times.

John chapter 21

The Ascension into Heaven

It was finally time for Jesus to leave the world for good. He gathered his disciples together and walked to the Mount of Olives, a short way from Jerusalem.

"Stay in the city for a while," Jesus told His eleven old friends. "You have already all been baptized once – by John the Baptist,

with water. But soon you will all be
baptized again – this time with the Holy
Spirit. God is going to send you powerful
gifts and I want you to use them by going
out into the world and telling people in
every country about me. Baptize all those
who believe in me as my followers, in the
name of the Father, the Son and the Holy
Spirit. Teach them everything that I have
taught you." Jesus looked at His friends'
worried faces. "Don't forget," He said
gently, "I will be with you always, until the
end of time."

With that, Jesus rose up into the air,
higher and higher, until He disappeared
into a blazing cloud of glory.

As the disciples squinted up at the

dazzling light, it glimmered, gleamed and then faded... Jesus was gone but they carried on gazing up at the empty blue sky.

"Men of Galilee, what are you looking at?" came a voice. The disciples turned to find two men in glowing robes standing next to them.

"Jesus has gone, but one day He will come back to you in the same way."

Full of wonder and sadness, the disciples were comforted and made their way back to Jerusalem. They knew they would not see Jesus again soon, but were sure that one day He would return in glory.

Matthew chapter 28; Mark chapter 16; Luke chapter 24; Acts chapter 1

The Coming of the Holy Spirit

The disciples were in Jerusalem waiting for the Holy Spirit to come and baptize them, as Jesus had told them. Meanwhile they decided to replace the traitor, Judas Iscariot, with a new disciple. Then they would be twelve once more, as Jesus had originally intended. They prayed for guidance, and cast votes and Matthias was chosen. The twelve became known as the apostles. Then the waiting continued.

Fifty days after Passover and the death of Jesus, it was the feast of Pentecost – when Jews celebrated how God had given their religious laws to Moses. The apostles were celebrating the feast, when suddenly a mighty sound like a rushing wind filled their ears as though it was all around them in the house. The apostles felt alive and full of energy, and turning to each other in astonishment, they saw that every man had a tiny flame hovering over his head.

"It must be the Holy Spirit!" they cried, and they found they were all speaking in different languages.

Realizing they had been blessed with the special gifts Jesus had talked about, the apostles excitedly ran out into the streets. Some found themselves giving thanks to God in Greek. Others were preaching about Jesus in Latin. Some were praising the Holy Spirit in Arabic, and many other languages.

Worshippers from foreign lands had come to Jerusalem for Pentecost and they were stunned. "These men are from Galilee!" they marvelled. "How can they speak our language?"

However, some people just laughed and said that the apostles were drunk.

Then Peter began preaching and everyone who heard him was stirred by his passion. "We are not drunk," he laughed. "We are followers of Jesus of Nazareth. He has risen from the dead, we have seen it with our own eyes. Today we have been blessed by the Holy Spirit with these gifts of languages. Anyone who is truly sorry for their sins and follows the teachings of Jesus will be blessed too. Who wants to join us?"

That day the apostles baptized over three thousand people as followers of Jesus. The foundations of the Christian Church had been laid.

Acts chapters 1, 2